T.H. MEYER was born in S the founder and publisher of Perseus Verlag, Basel, and editor of the monthly journals *Der Europäer* and *The Present Age*. He is the author of several books including *Ludwig Polzer-Hoditz, A Biography*; *D.N. Dunlop, A Biography*; *Rudolf Steiner's Core Mission*; *The Bodhisattva Question*; *Clairvoyance and Consciousness* and *Reality, Truth and Evil*, and editor of *Light for the New Millennium*. He has written numerous articles and gives seminars and lectures around the world.

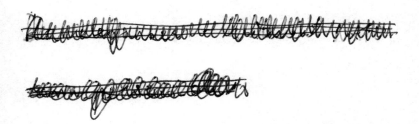

IN THE SIGN OF FIVE

1879 – 1899 – 1933 – 1998 – Today

The Five Spiritual Events, Tasks and Beings of the First Half of the Age of Michael

An Apocalyptic View of Contemporary History

T.H. Meyer

TEMPLE LODGE

Temple Lodge Publishing Ltd.
Hillside House, The Square
Forest Row, RH18 5ES

www.templelodge.com

First published in English by Temple Lodge Publishing, 2015

Originally published in German under the title *Im Zeichen der Fünf* by Perseus Verlag, Basel, 2014

Translated from German by Terry M. Boardman

© Perseus Verlag 2014
This translation © Temple Lodge Publishing 2015

The right of T.H. Meyer to be identified as the author of this work has been asserted in accordance with sections 77 and 78 of the Copyright, Designs and Patents Act, 1988

A CIP catalogue record for this book is available from the British Library

ISBN 978 1 906999 79 7

Cover by Morgan Creative featuring detail from *The Resurrected One* by Vincenzo Foppa
Typeset by DP Photosetting, Neath, West Glamorgan
Printed and bound by 4Edge Ltd.

Contents

For a while now — especially since the beginning of the twentieth century — or more accurately, since the year 1899, we have been standing within a new wave of spiritual life, which has been pouring itself into the rest of human life. And a spiritual researcher is today only a human being who acknowledges this, that is, who notices that this has broken into the life of mankind.

That is the one fact.

The other fact is that human beings, precisely because of their present constitution, need a certain bestirring of themselves, a certain activity, in order to notice that such a wave has been pouring itself into life. [...] the human being can resist acknowledging this in his consciousness, but he cannot prevent his soul from feeling the impact of this wave or from feeling that it is within him.

Rudolf Steiner, Lecture on New Year's Day 1919, GA 187[*]

---

[*] GA = *Gesamtausgabe* or Collected Works. See Bibliography on p. 92.

Preface

This short text addresses in an aphoristic form the five most important spiritual events since 1879, the beginning of the Age of Michael, which will last for about 350 years. It does this against the background of the main task of our 5th post-Atlantean Epoch, which began in 1413 and will continue until 3573: the epistemological struggle with evil. The considerations in this book will be presented on the basis of the spiritual science developed by Rudolf Steiner.

The five events of the present Age of Michael are linked with the years 1879, 1899, 1933, 1998, and the present time. Expressed in concise phrases, these are: the rise of Michael to the rank of Time Spirit (1879); the end of Kali Yuga (1899); the appearance of Christ in the Etheric (1933); the assault of Sorath (1998) — 'one of the greatest ahrimanic demons', according to Rudolf Steiner; and finally, the incarnation of Ahriman at the present time.

On closer consideration, these events show themselves to be linked to five *fundamental tasks* of the Age of Michael. All five tasks depend essentially on the great epistemological challenge of the 5th post-Atlantean Epoch as a whole. Behind the five events stand certain *spiritual beings*: Michael, Christ, Sorath, and Ahriman, while the beings who brought about the event of 1899 remain more hidden. The question is: how far were the tasks presented by these essential events recognized, and how far were they carried out?

In the light of world history and within the organism of the five events, we stand today at the fifth place — at the point of the incarnation of Ahriman. Who is prepared for this decisive event? Can one be prepared for it who knows nothing of it? Is it necessarily so, on the other hand, that all are prepared who know something about it?

The phenomena of evil surround us daily. But are they

recognized? And how does evil relate to the good guidance of the world, such as there is? How does it relate to the Michael or to the Christ impulse, the most important of the five events to be described? Can one speak as a serious contemporary of the 'banality of evil', as the cultural philosopher Hannah Arendt did?

And once again, the key spiritual question of the present time: how well or how poorly prepared are human beings today for the event of the incarnation of Ahriman in the West, of which Rudolf Steiner spoke in a series of lectures almost 100 years ago?

*

The world seems to be standing within a demonic storm which threatens to overwhelm it. Whoever has stood before the representation of St Anthony on the Isenheim altar at Colmar (or who knows it from reproductions) can experience what not only St Anthony went through, but that which every human soul today who strives for spiritual knowledge has to undergo. No appeal to traditional religious beliefs will pacify this storm. Nor will 'good will' any longer suffice, unless this good will shows itself to be a will for uncompromising knowledge. This can only result from a wide-ranging spiritual-scientific observation of the world—one for which world history is something very different from the 'fable convenue' of which Napoleon rightly spoke. Such a view of the world shows that behind all phenomenal appearances in the world are *beings* (*Wesenheiten*) which are of a supersensible, *spiritual* nature. To be able to orient oneself in the confusion and darkness of our time, even only in an approximate manner, an urgent need of the hour is to learn about these beings in the most comprehensive manner possible. Neither economic nor political struggles, not even the wars, more or less restricted to certain regions, which take place across the globe—nothing of any of these has to do with the core of the deeper events of our time. This core consists in the struggle of human souls for a true knowledge of the spirit. In terms of world history, this is already present in a homeopathic potency, through the creative deed of

Rudolf Steiner. Goethe's great words apply to the fruits of this deed: 'You must *earn* what you have received from your fathers in order to possess it.' Steiner's spiritual heritage must be 'earned'. Otherwise it will rot away as 'mere knowledge', or else fall into the hands of thieves who will abuse it.

Spiritual knowledge is not given to us as in ancient times. By spiritual means it must be struggled and striven for against a host of demons, as St Anthony had to do. We must therefore get to know the powers that would cover over and obscure all spiritual knowledge. These are in the first place today the hosts of Ahriman and Sorath. Developing our knowledge of these in the light of Michael and of the new Christ Event can lead to spiritual victories which appear in the present climate of spiritual denial to be not exactly prevalent...

*

The facts, beings, and problems addressed in this book are therefore complex and take many forms, and it is hoped that the reader will be able to exercise much cognitive patience. As the five events and beings described in the book and the tasks associated with them are, as already mentioned, all embedded in the fundamental task of the fifth post-Atlantean Epoch, this fundamental task forms the subject of the first chapter.

The reader who would like a more comprehensive overview *before* considering the five events and tasks may refer to the considerations in Chapter IX, 'The Development of Mankind in the Course of a Cosmic Year' (p. 79). This will make clear and comprehensible the cosmic origin, so to speak, of the appearance of spiritual science within the whole context of the development of mankind. It is no accident that knowledge of the spirit appeared in the same 'moment' in world history in which mankind was called to solve the riddle of the knowledge of evil, and indeed to a 'scientific' solution of this riddle, as Steiner emphasized on 3 November 1917. Without a concrete spiritual science this riddle cannot be answered. This is also known to certain occultists who therefore wish to keep spiritual science away from mankind or to reveal it only in a veiled or caricatured form so that mankind will all the more fall into evil, lose all restraint and orientation, and *thereby remain beholden to the spiritual or economic powers of leadership of these occultists.* Steiner also emphasized this in a lecture on *Faust*, 28 September 1918, GA 273.

*

The five events, tasks, and beings will be discussed not so much in a chronological, linear fashion as in layered dimensions. Many points will thereby be encompassed and illuminated from different sides so that there will be certain overlaps, which, viewed superficially, may appear to be repetitive, but they were deliberately not omitted. In the core thematic Chapters III and IV, longer sub-sections have been added for ease of understanding and overview and have been included in the Contents. In the other chapters there are also short sub-sections, but for the sake of simplicity their titles appear only in the chapters themselves.

*

For the reader who seriously wishes to go further into the deeper or higher issues discussed in this book, the words which Benedictus speaks in Steiner's Mystery Drama *The Soul's Probation*, point a way forward:

> Paths to higher truth are confusing.
> Only he can find his way rightly
> Who has patience to wander through labyrinths.

Thomas Meyer
Barr, 21 January 2014

I. THE FUNDAMENTAL QUESTION OF THE FIFTH POST-ATLANTEAN EPOCH

'In the spirit is harmony.'

Daily verse by Rudolf Steiner for Friday

'One will not understand relationships in world evolution if one does not make use of the principle of number as a method of investigation.'

Rudolf Steiner on 17 September 1924, GA 346

Mankind finds itself in the fifth post-Atlantean Epoch which began in 1413 and will end in 3573. The period of 2160 years between the beginning and end of this period is an astronomic heavenly number: in the course of this period the vernal point appears to retrogress through a Zodiac sign. One speaks of the precession of the vernal (spring) point. Since 1413 it has been in the sign of the Fishes (Pisces); the year 3573 will mark the beginning of the sign of the Water-bearer (Aquarius).[1] The fourth post-Atlantean Epoch occurred in the sign of the Ram (Aries), the third in the sign of the Bull (Taurus), the second in the sign of the Twins (Gemini), and the first post-Atlantean Epoch occurred in the sign of the Crab (Cancer).

Each of these epochs has quite distinct fundamental tasks. Only the fundamental tasks of the fourth and fifth post-Atlantean Epochs will be briefly outlined. In the Greco-Roman epoch, the riddle to be tackled was that of birth and death, or of human mortality. This riddling question created a certain insecurity in human feelings which needed to be addressed. 'Better a beggar in the upper world than a king in the lower', goes the well-known saying of the Greek poet Homer, which points to the threatening uncertainty about life after death (the lower world).

*

The consciousness of human immortality began to darken. The destiny of the human soul seemed more and more subject to impenetrable and even blind divine powers. This is evident in the great tragedies of the Greek dramatists. Only the Event of Golgotha brought new light. Christ did not only ascend to heavenly heights as portrayed in Matthias Grünewald's painting of the Resurrection in Colmar; as light-bringer, He also descended into the underworld which had become dark. He brought light into the karma of the individual human soul and its life after death. The relationship between this earthly life and life after death was illumined. Christ became the incarnate solution to the fundamental riddle of the fourth post-Atlantean Epoch.

Evil and the Knowledge of it

The fundamental task of the fifth post-Atlantean Epoch is quite different. It is: *understanding evil and its origins in a higher Good.* Rudolf Steiner represented this double task and especially the question of the higher, *ethical origin* of evil in monumental simplicity in his second Mystery Drama, *The Soul's Probation.* He did this in the form of a fairy tale which shows 'how evil can arise from Good'. This fairy tale was also included in a collection of texts which Helene Röchling, the great benefactor of the first Goetheanum building, sponsored as 'a gift of love for German POWs'.[2]

The short fairy tale was printed in the collection with the simple title 'Where Does Evil Come From?'. This question touched and touches the hearts of countless contemporaries then and now. No wonder that it touches on the fundamental question and fundamental task of the present Age of the Fishes (Pisces).[3]

It is no accident that Rudolf Steiner repeatedly sketched this fundamental task in his lectures about Goethe's *Faust* in the year 1917 – a year of great significance in world history. Goethe can therefore be regarded as *the* poet of the fundamental task of the fifth post-Atlantean Epoch.

In a lecture in Dornach on 3 November 1917 Steiner said:

We, the people of the fifth post-Atlantean Epoch, [...] have to solve
the problem of evil, to the widest extent possible and in a living and
powerful way. [...] Evil, which will impose itself on the human being
in this fifth post-Atlantean Epoch in every form possible, and will
impose itself in such a way that the human being will have to
comprehend the nature and the being of evil so that in his loves and
hates he can cope with everything that comes at him that is of an evil
nature, so that he can fight and struggle against the resistance that
evil puts up against his will impulses — all this belongs to the tasks of
the fifth post-Atlantean Epoch.[4]

Evil and the Interior of the Earth

For a cognitive confrontation with evil, knowledge of the nine
layers of the interior of the Earth is necessary. It is from these
layers that the impulses of evil, anti-divine impulses ray out, so
to speak. Although Rudolf Steiner pointed to this hard-to-access
but significant area of research and gave a spiritual-ethical outline of the layers of the Earth, the field has been little studied
until today.[5] Adolf Arenson and Sigismund von Gleich are two
great exceptions. There is, however, a lack of contemporary
indications of comparable depth regarding this field, which is so
closely related to the fundamental task of the fifth post-Atlantean
Epoch; what exists is mostly presented without the necessary
factual reference being made to the efforts of these two pupils of
Rudolf Steiner.

Evil, Freedom and Love

The higher goal of the confrontation with evil that is a need of our
times is an intensification of the 'the spiritual life of the Good', a
human step forward on freedom's path of development and a
higher development of the capacity for love. Evil, love, and
freedom are inseparable from each other in the development of
mankind, like the three corners of a triangle.[6] One who only
wishes to focus on the 'love angle' and the 'freedom angle' of the
triangle but who eliminates 'the angle of evil' would thereby
eliminate the whole triangle of development itself.

'... *it* **must** *be revealed'*

In the same period during the First World War Steiner once expressed himself in a personal conversation in another, very incisive fashion.

This was in conversation with Adelheid Petersen, the leader of the Munich branch of the Anthroposophical Society and from whom, as far as we know, stems the best synopsis of the reincarnational aspects of Steiner's Mystery Dramas.[7] Petersen reports:

> On a dull February morning [in 1915] walking up to the Goetheanum I met Rudolf Steiner. The dull thump of artillery fire was audible from Alsace. Sometimes, after one particularly heavy blast, the ground shook. Rudolf Steiner stood there for a long time, looking over to the West, which was covered in a damp mist. Then he looked at me with that indescribable gaze which went right into one's depths but without penetration, without any sharpness; a gaze which did not seek to grasp but which rested in itself. 'Yes', he said finally, 'when that over there', he gestured to the West, 'when that over there comes to an end, then everything will be so utterly different from what it was before, that you would not understand me if I tried to tell you how it will be. But you will experience it! When it is over, what they are calling war—yes, then everything conventional will break down; all the whitewash will fall away from relationships in life! Humankind has entered upon a stage of its development in which evil and lies must become visible! It is all there already: evil, cruelty, falsehood, decay—it is all there, but it is still whitewashed over! And it *must* be revealed! It will show itself in individuals' relationships—in marriages, families, friendships, and above all in enmities—just as in the collective life of peoples, of states! For certain things there will be no more limits.

And after this unsparing diagnostic look into the abyss of the times, Steiner gave Petersen, and with her, all real contemporaries, a fundamental therapeutic piece of advice in order to enable them to withstand the great challenge:

> Only those people will be able to endure everything that is approaching without going under in their souls, without being

damaged in their souls, who are able to distinguish what is essential
from what is inessential outside themselves and above all, in their
own inner life! That is very hard! Very hard!', he repeated, 'it calls for
constant, courageous practice. For here lies the most dreadful
temptation! Mankind will have to struggle against the Lie—the
primal evil!' He turned to walk to the (Goetheanum) building. The
sound of the mallets on the wooden grips of the chisels rang out in
various tones, bright and dark, high and low, ringing or dull, almost
like bells ringing. Rudolf Steiner smiled: the happiness and all the
love of a great creator standing before his work radiated from him.[8]

A Fundamental Distinction

In March 1909 Rudolf Steiner gave a fundamental indication
about the knowledge of evil which will be discussed in detail
later, and only briefly mentioned here because of its great significance. It has to do with the need for a clear distinction
between time and eternity, soul and spirit. One who fails to make
this distinction will perhaps believe, precisely when observing
difficult current events, that there could be both an eternal good
as well as an 'eternal evil'. This is not the case. Certainly one can
and should speak of an eternal good, but to say the same of evil is
as meaningless as speaking of wooden iron. According to
Steiner, 'One who does not rise from the temporal to the eternal
never understands evil'.[9]

This distinction is, as we hope to be able to show, one of the
most important preconditions for a contemporary, reasoned
understanding of evil. It was a pathfinder for everything the
author has written in this book.

II. LARGER AND SMALLER CYCLES OF DEVELOPMENT IN THE SIGN OF FIVE

The fifth post-Atlantean Epoch in which we are now living and which will last 2160 years in total began, as already mentioned, in 1413. The year 1413 in turn lay in the middle of a *smaller* cycle of 320–50 years. There are seven of these smaller cycles and they are ruled by the following Time Spirit Archangels who, in the sequence of their activity, are: Oriphiel, Anael, Zachariel, Raphael, Samael, Gabriel, and Michael. The sequence of the archangels corresponds to the planetary spheres to which they belong: Saturn, Venus, Jupiter, Mercury, Mars, Moon, Sun, or, beginning with Saturday, the retrogression of the seven days of the week.[10]

Samael, the Archangel of the Mars sphere, stands in the *fifth* position in the sequence, which begins with Oriphiel. We can see from the foregoing that the fifth post-Atlantean Epoch began during a *fifth* small cycle, thus during a Samael regency. In schools of occult wisdom one would have said of this, in 'shorthand', that it began in 5/5. The small Samael period thereby engraved its quite distinctive signature on the larger, fifth post-Atlantean Epoch *from the very beginning.* In his lectures on the Apocalypse which he gave to the priests of the Christian Community in September 1924 and which, in parallel with the last karma lectures, the drama course and those on pastoral medicine, crowned his work as a lecturer and served as a kind of legacy-like character to them, Rudolf Steiner referred to this 5/5 signature on 10 September 1924: 'When an epoch begins with Mars forces [...] there is something warlike in it'; and further: in this combative beginning there is already the prophetic indication about *the end of the fifth* great age of the earth, which lasts seven times 2160 years, that is, 15,120 years, and after the end of the seventh post-Atlantean Epoch, it will lead the Earth over into the sixth great age of the Earth. This present fifth great age will end with 'the war of all against all' which will take place in the seventh post-Atlantean Epoch. 'The fifth [post-Atlantean] cultural epoch', said Steiner,

> began with what came from Mars through Samael, the spirit of strife, in that elements of strife were brought down from the spiritual world. And at the beginning of the epoch of the consciousness soul we see how in this smaller cycle [the Samael cycle] our fifth epoch contains in itself something of the portent, the prophetic portent of how the great epoch will end, after the fifth [post-Atlantean] cultural epoch is followed by the sixth and seventh epochs.

*

Within the *fifth* great Earth epoch, we are therefore living in the *fifth* cultural epoch which began with the regency of the *fifth* Archangel. *The year 1413 therefore fell in a triple fivefoldness: 5/5/5.*

The seven Earth Epochs
1. Polarian / 2. Hyperborean / 3. Lemurian / 4. Atlantean / 5. Post-Atlantean / 6. Earth epoch / 7. Earth epoch

The Seven Cultural Periods of the Post-Atlantean Epoch
Length: 7 × 2160 years = 15120 years
1. Indian / 2. Persian / 3. Egypto-Chaldean / 4. Greco-Roman / 5. Germanic-Anglo-Saxon / 6. Slavic / 7. American
The fifth post-Atlantean period began in 1413, in the sign of the Fishes (Pisces).

The Seven Archangelic Periods
Length: 7 × c. 354 years
Oriphiel 250 BC–150 AD / Anael 150–500 / Zachariel 500–850 / Raphael 850–1190 / Samael 1190–1510 / Gabriel 1510–1879 / Michael 1879–2230

The fifth post-Atlantean Epoch began within an Age of Samael, the regency of the fifth Archangel.

Fig 1   *The Three Layers of Time in Relation to the 5/5/5*

The Number Five, considered qualitatively

If we accept that the number five, qualitatively considered, both according to ancient occult tradition and in the sense of modern spiritual science, is called the number of evil or of decision, we shall not be surprised that the great spiritual cultural task in the fifth post-Atlantean Epoch is *the confrontation with evil* described in the first chapter (while that of the fourth cultural epoch, as also mentioned there, was the confrontation with the riddle of birth and death).

Steiner also describes the number five as the number of 'crisis', which shows itself in the course of illnesses. The anthroposophical mathematician Ernst Bindel also speaks of five as the number of the 'creative individual'.[11] All these aspects are related in that with the emergence of the *fifth* element in the human organism, the Spirit-Self, the capacities for freedom and love, but also the tendency towards evil, all appear in new ways that had never before existed.

'When one relates number to what goes on', said Steiner in his 1924 lectures to the priests, 'then one learns, as it were, to read the World-All apocalyptically, and one will find everywhere that countless secrets reveal themselves to one who learns to observe the world apocalyptically in this way'.

This book seeks to make a contribution to such an apocalyptic mode of observation, especially in regard to the fifth event of the current Age of Michael, the incarnation of Ahriman in the West.

III. THE FIRST FIVE EVENTS OF THE CURRENT AGE OF MICHAEL

Today we are living in the *seventh* small archangelic period within the fifth post-Atlantean Epoch; we can express this in abbreviated form as 5/7. This seventh smaller period is the Age of Michael, which began in 1879.

A seventh smaller period always brings with it certain impulses, both positive and negative, as high points and low points.

The present Age of Michael has been characterized thus far by *five* great spiritual events. The mere relating of the dates in which these events have fallen can already reveal to the observer familiar with spiritual science something of the spiritual span of this Michael Age. These dates are: 1879, 1899, 1933, 1998, and today. This spectrum of events becomes all the more expressive when we refer even superficially to the spiritual events that have occurred at these times: the rise of the Archangel Michael to the rank of Time Spirit (1879), the end of the Kali Yuga period (1899), the beginning of the etheric appearance of Christ (1933), the third manifestation of the activity of Sorath, who is the cosmic opponent of Christ (1998), and finally the incarnation of Ahriman 'before even a part of the third millennium of the Christian era has run its course'.[12]

The five events all fall in the current Michael Age. That these so completely different processes all occur in the first half of our Michael Age characterizes this Michael Age and the Michael Spirit leading it much more concretely than would be possible through any kind of direct conceptual discussion of the being of Michael, for theoretically, the five events could have been shared out among different archangelic ages by the spiritual guidance of the world. However, it was evidently the intention of the spiritual leaders of mankind to have them all occur during the first half of the current Age of Michael.

We therefore have to observe a series of spiritual *events* behind which stand quite definite spiritual *beings* who call mankind to equally definite spiritual *tasks*, and these tasks are at the same time Michaelic tasks, for they are placed precisely in this Michael Age.

These *events* will now be briefly characterized. The sketch of the first two events will be accompanied by a brief look at parallel developments in the life of Rudolf Steiner. Later, we shall consider the *tasks* that arise in relation to these events. Finally, we shall take a closer look at the spiritual beings associated with these events and tasks.

1. The Beginning of the Age of Michael in November 1879

The first spiritual event is of course the beginning of the Age of Michael itself. It occurred exactly at the time of the first Moon Node which the young Rudolf Steiner experienced shortly after his arrival in Vienna in autumn 1879.

Steiner was therefore a direct witness in his soul and spirit of the beginning of the new Age of Michael. At this time also occurred Steiner's meeting with one of his 'Masters', if not with both of them.[13] This meeting planted the seed for a comprehensive spiritualization of his intellect, as is shown in Steiner's basic work *The Philosophy of Spiritual Activity*, from which resulted a spiritual observation of the evolution of the world and mankind, as was later expressed in his *Occult Science: An Outline*. How far *The Philosophy of Spiritual Activity* was Steiner's first and actual Michaelic work will be briefly discussed later. First, it should be pointed out that it was the only one of his works which is mentioned in his last written work, the so-called *Anthroposophical Leading Thoughts*, at the centre of which are considerations about Michael.

Symptomatic of one of the tasks of the Age of Michael which will be discussed in more detail later is the fact, noted by W.J. Stein, that in 1879 the concept of the *world economy* first made its appearance. Here the cosmopolitan element is evident, as well as the task of needing to enter into the most earthly realities in accordance with spiritual perspectives.

During his lifetime (1861–1925) Steiner was not only a witness of the first and second events in the early Age of Michael but was also a herald of the three later events.

2. The End of Kali Yuga on 19 February 1899

In 1899 the 5,000 year-long Age of Darkness (Kali Yuga) came to an end; according to one indication by Elisabeth Vreede this occurred on 19 February 1899.[14]

As the concept of Kali Yuga is less familiar to the Western spiritual seeker than that of a new Age of Michael, it will be outlined a little further here. For 5,000 years, mankind had developed from the condition of ancient clairvoyance into one of grasping the physical world through the senses and the intellect. Indian tradition sees the beginning of Kali Yuga at the time of the 'death' of the god Krishna in 3101 BC. The *Bhagavad Gita* relates how Krishna first instructs the hero Arjuna that spiritual truths are no longer to be merely inspirational or imaginative but are to be grasped by means of pure thinking. So in the Second Song comes the great teaching of the immortality of the human soul *in the form of thoughts*—a revolutionary innovation for that time. Pure thinking emerged as the final remnant, or as the newest transformative product of the old imaginative and inspirational clairvoyance. It rose up into the same, light spiritual heights from which earlier Intuitions, Inspirations and Imaginations had streamed down into human consciousness.

In the course of 5,000 years, human thinking sank from the exalted heights of its origins down into a mere grasping of material sense reality. Over many centuries this certainly enabled the development of natural science and technology, but in its devotion to grasping the world of the senses, thinking was threatened with the loss of its own spiritual origin.

In the middle of this developmental crisis of human thinking, which had originally been born of the spirit, with the end of Kali Yuga—hardly 20 years after the end of the Age of Michael—came the turning point towards a new *Age of Light*.

In Rudolf Steiner's development the years 1898–9 likewise

show a spiritual turning point. In his autobiography *Mein Lebensgang* [The Course of My Life] he speaks of a

> struggle against demonic powers which wanted to facilitate not a spiritual way of seeing in understanding nature but a mechanistic-naturalistic way of thinking. [...] At that time I had to save my spiritual vision in the midst of inner storms [...]. Before the turn of the century my soul was tested as described. My soul development came to the point where, in spirit, I stood before the Mystery of Golgotha in a most intimate, most solemn celebration of knowledge.

The 26th chapter of *The Course of My Life* closes with the last two sentences, and the following three sentences introduce the 27th chapter: 'It was clear to me then that the turn of the century would bring a new spiritual light to mankind. It seemed to me that the isolation of human thinking and will from the spirit had reached a peak. A turnaround in mankind's path of development seemed to me to be a necessity.'

3. The Reappearance of Christ in the Etheric from 1933

Steiner referred to this third, most important spiritual event in general form from 1909 onwards. He spoke about it quite unequivocally on 12 January 1910 in a special lecture in Stockholm to members of the Theosophical Society. This 'happened to be' the same day which in Adyar (India) saw completion of the 'initiation' of Krishnamurti, who was presented by leading Theosophists there as the physically reincarnated Bodhisattva or Christ – no clear distinction was made between the two beings.[15]

No stenographic record has survived of the Stockholm lecture. Only some notes by Marie von Sivers provide some information about it in the form of abbreviated phrases.[16] First she wrote: '3000 BC Kali Yuga began, lasted till 1899'. According to the brief notes by Marie von Sivers, it was foreseen that the Reappearance of Christ would take place in the year 1933. Later, a few years were grouped around 1933.

Further elements relating to this first direct indication of the Reappearance of Christ will be discussed in Chapter IV.

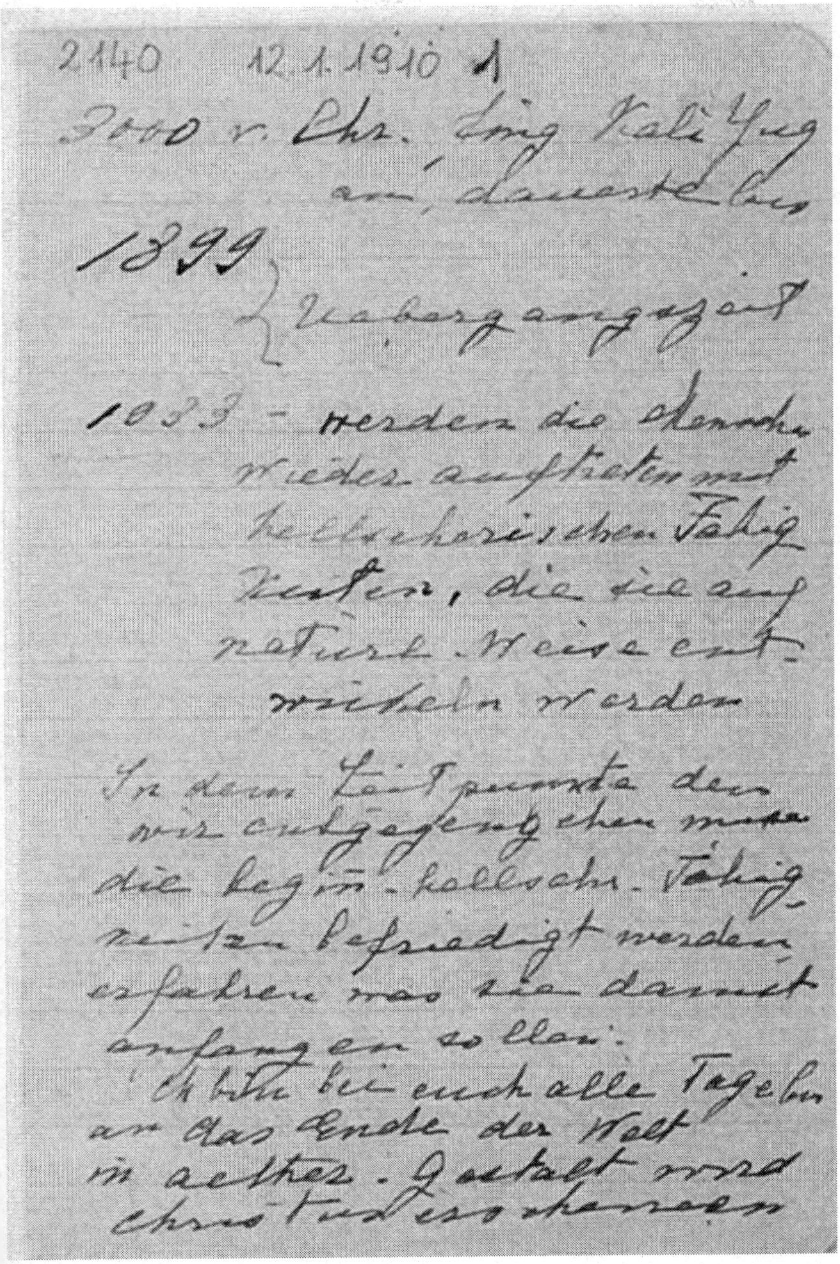
2140 12.1.1910 1
3000 v. Chr. Beginn Kali Yug
am Ende bis
1899
} Uebergangszeit
1933 – werden die Menschen
wieder auftreten mit
hellseherischen Fähig
keiten, die sie auf
natürl. Weise ent-
wickeln werden
In dem Zeitpunkte dem
wir entgegengehen muss
die begin. hellsehr. Fähig-
keiten befriedigt werden
erfahren was sie damit
anfangen sollen.
'Ich bin bei euch alle Tage bis
an das Ende der Welt
in aether. Gestalt wird
Christus erscheinen

Fig 2 Excerpt from Notes by Marie von Sivers, 12 January 1910

3000   BC Kali Yuga began, lasted till 1899
       Time of transition

1933 — people will emerge again with clairvoyant capacities, which
       will develop in natural ways.

In the times we are approaching, emergent clairvoyant faculties will
have to be encountered and experienced which they [people] will
have to begin to do.
I am with you all always to the end of the world.
Christ will appear in etheric form. The physical Christ became the
spirit of our Earth — that was the mid-point, the fulcrum, of Earth
development.
5 Letter of the Ap[ocalypse]: I shall come, but be alert lest you do not
recognize me.
Mankind has 2,500 years to redevelop clairvoyant gifts. Around 1933
the Gospels must be so well understood in their spiritual sense that
they will have worked to prepare the way for Christ. Otherwise,
there would be unending confusion of the soul.
Around 1933 there will be emissaries from black magic schools who
will falsely proclaim a physical Christ.
Every time Christ is supposed to be perceptible, he is perceptible for
other capacities.

Fig 3   Translation of Notes by Marie von Sivers

The Reappearance of Christ in the Etheric as well as the two
following events announced by Steiner were not experienced by
him on the physical plane.

4. The Attack of Sorath in 1998 and its Precursors in the Twentieth Century

The fourth event is the renewed incursion into the course of
history by one of 'the most powerful demons in our [solar] system', one of the 'greatest ahrimanic demons', who is related to
the number 666 and who bears the name Sorath. Rudolf Steiner
also calls him the 'Sun-Demon'. For the audience of priests at his
lectures on the Apocalypse (GA 346) in 1924 he drew the occult

sign for this demon on the blackboard, as he had done before during the Apocalypse cycle lectures in Nuremberg in 1908. Observation of this sign can reveal much of its spiritual nature, which is also true in the most positive sense for the signs of Christ and Michael (see p. 61 ff.).

In the Apocalypse lectures for the priests Steiner refers to the year 1998 as the third 'Sorath year' of the Christian era. Anti-spiritual impulses of the strongest kind are associated with every one of these Sorath years.

The first Sorath year, 666, is related to the Academy of Gon-dishapur, the activities of which were intended to bring about a premature development of human intellectuality; this was prevented and dampened down by the impulse of Mohammed (Islam).

In the period before the second Sorath year (2 × 666), the Order of the Knights Templar was destroyed by King Philip the Fair of France and Pope Clement V who was beholden to him; 'confessions' obtained under torture (and later mostly recanted) were used to convict the Templars, who were arrested in a *coup de main* which took place throughout France on a single night. In the period around the third Sorath year of 1998 the great world catastrophe of 9/11[17] took place, 77 years after Steiner's momentous revelations about Sorath in September 1924. This resulted in acts of torture committed worldwide by the regime of the US military junta in the name of 'the War on Terror', which were supposed to secure the conviction of the perpetrators of terrorism and which in their cruelty were on a par with the tortures committed against the Templars.

1914–33: *The Preludes to the Third Sorath Attack*

In his lectures to the priests on the subject of the Apocalypse, Rudolf Steiner indicated that there would be grim preludes to the third attack by Sorath. The first had played itself out at the time of the outbreak of the First World War; Steiner saw the second in Bolshevism, which burst upon the world in 1917. We can see a third prelude in Hitler's seizure of power in 1933 and its consequences.

On 12 September 1924 Steiner said to the priests (GA 346): 'The way will be paved for the entry of the demons which are the servants of the great demon Sorath.'

> One only needs to speak to informed people who, for example, know something about the outbreak of the First World War. One will not be wrong when one says that of the approximately 40 individuals who were responsible for the outbreak of the war, almost all of them were in a state of lowered consciousness at the time. That is always the point of entry for ahrimanic demonic powers, and one of the greatest of these demons is Sorath. They are the attempts from the side of Sorath to penetrate, at least temporarily at first, into human consciousness and to bring disaster and confusion.

On 31 May 1924 in the 14th Class Lesson, Steiner had already given an indication in just this same direction. He spoke then too of the 30–40 individuals who had taken part in the outbreak of the war and who 'at the decisive moment had a clouded consciousness'. He even stated that precisely in this regard, an adequate history of the war could never be written on the basis of documented outer facts *alone*. 'This war can only be written in an occult sense.'[18] A statement to be taken especially seriously in the 100th year since the outbreak of the war!

In the lectures to the priests in September 1924, the ahrimanic spirituality that was active in the world war was described as sorathic-ahrimanic. It was not the war as such that should be seen as the work of Sorath — it had causes that had to do with world karma which to a considerable extent were to be traced back to the division of East and West that was initiated by Rome in the ninth century — but rather, 'what followed it and which is dreadful and will become even more dreadful, for example the present condition of Russia, that is something which the Sorath spirits pressing into human souls are striving for'. The rising tide of Bolshevism therefore, together with its gulags that showed themselves later, were described as sorathic — that is, radically anti-human and anti-spiritual.

The same must be said in regard to the world-historical events of the year 1933: National Socialism and its anti-human institutions and activities were ahrimanic and sorathic in nature, apart from the more luciferic pomp and display, which, for example, was on show at the cultic Nazi Party rallies. 'One will see people', said Steiner on 12 September 1924, 'whom one cannot believe are actually human. Outwardly, they will have intensely strong natures with violent dispositions, a destructive will in their emotions [...] they will pour scorn in the most appalling manner on everything spiritual and fight against it and throw it on to the fire.' Such people did appear during the 12 year-long horror of the Nazi regime; they appeared during the 70 year-long nightmare of Bolshevism. And Steiner prophesied that what was concentrated 'in its core' in Bolshevism at that time, 'would be inserted into the whole earthly development of mankind'. Doubtless this also applies to what was 'concentrated' in Nazism. The same could be said with regard to developments in China and other states in Asia.

All of this, however, represented 'only' a kind of variegated prelude to the main attack around the year 1998. Now the human beings inspired by Sorath appeared more within the Americanism that had risen to world power since 1945 and which is concerned — and from the world-historical perspective indeed *must* be concerned — to ensure that the sorathic seeds of earthly development that were sown in Bolshevism and Nazism are permanently incorporated in this development; in other words, that the formation of the two sole remaining great 'Races' of the sixth Great Earth Epoch will actually be accomplished — that of spiritually oriented human individualities and that which rages in fury against everything which is of a spiritual nature.

1933 and the Beast from the Earth

In his Apocalypse lectures of September 1924 Steiner revealed something that was of great significance with regard to the year 1933. He indicated that the 'beasts' in the Apocalypse always have to do with comets and their appearances. Some comets have favourable effects, others negative effects. Such negative effects would have stemmed from a particular comet which, if it had turned up at the time calculated for it, would have destroyed the Earth in the year 1933, but it did not do so because it had broken apart earlier. This indeed happened but, because of it, the Earth was permeated by the substance of the comet which then rose up out of the Earth in the year 1933 — as the substance of the *two-horned beast*.

So the year 1933 was both the year of the Etheric Christ and also the year of the strongest prelude to the third world-historical attack by Sorath which culminated in 1998. More of this later.

Sympathy for the Devil

Rudolf Steiner already indicated in Stockholm in 1910 that 'around 1933 there will be envoys of black magic schools who will announce the false appearance of a physical Christ'. Such teachings about Christ one can find among Seventh Day Adventists, so-called Evangelical Christians, and Mormons. In addition, one can speak of a perverse tendency throughout the twentieth century to make sorathic evil ever more socially acceptable. Aleister Crowley, the English occultist with black magic inclinations and methods, can be regarded as a ground-breaker in this direction. Crowley identified himself with the 'Beast' from the Apocalypse. One of the founder members of the rock band the Rolling Stones, Mick Jagger, became interested in Crowley. Symptomatic of this deviant tendency was the band's song 'Sympathy for the Devil', which could be heard playing prior to Barack Obama's first public speech in Berlin before his election as US President.

Also in Berlin, in 1989, the year of 'the fall of the Wall', the 'Sorat' Hotel Group was founded; twelve hotels in Germany now bear the name 'Sorat'. The Group characterizes its hotels as 'individual city hotels with original ideas, a distinctive character and friendly service'. Charles Kovacs created a painting of Sorath which portrays in a masterly fashion the glisteningly seductive and utter heartlessness of the 'Beast' (see p. 57).[19]

5. The Incarnation of Ahriman in the West at the Beginning of the Third Millennium

The fifth spiritual event in the Age of Michael thus far is the incarnation of Ahriman in the West, which Rudolf Steiner spoke about in a series of lectures in the autumn of 1919 (see GA 191 and 193). This event falls at the beginning of the third millennium. Unlike the exact indications of time for all the previous four events, here we must be satisfied with an approximate indication but one which, seen in the context of the time, is yet quite precise, and which in any case has to do with the beginning of our millennium. This comes from the following indication by Rudolf Steiner on 1 November 1919. In this lecture, Steiner states that the incarnation of Ahriman will occur 'before even a part of the third millennium of the Christian era has run its course' (GA 191). This formulation points to the first decade of this millennium, if by 'part' one understands a hundredth of a millennium. It seems to us improbable that, by 'part', Steiner could have meant a tenth of the third millennium; if so, his prophecy would have referred in a vague fashion to the whole of the twenty-first century.

The Sorath attack of 1998 represents the direct historical prelude to the incarnation of Ahriman. It is the first and only incarnation of this being, comparable with the single incarnation of Lucifer in the third millennium BC and the Incarnation of Christ at the Turning Point of Time in Palestine.

Steiner indicated a whole series of phenomena and tendencies through which Ahriman has sought to prepare for his incarnation in ways that would be favourable for him.[20] The means by which, in Ahriman's sense, this incarnation can be most successfully prepared for are, amongst others: the spread of the ideology and practice of nationalism and racism; the belief in the omnipotent nature of statistical data, for example also in medical practice; political party management; a one-sided materialistic cosmology; the tendency to spiritual revelations that make no demands on the recipients, and the belief in the omnipotence of the unitary State. And last but not least: the false, that is, the literal understanding of the Gospels, uninformed by spiritual perspectives.

IV. THE FIVE SPIRITUAL TASKS

The five spiritual events outlined did not follow one another haphazardly. Even if it is still not possible today to indicate further spiritual events in what remains of the Age of Michael, the five events that have already occurred immediately show a certain structure which cannot be regarded as accidental. The first two and the last two are close to each other in time. The first two all too evidently bring a *positive* impulse for the whole future development of mankind; the last two represent hindrances against the realization of these impulses, and in this sense are not so much primary impulses like the first two but reactive impulses, as it were. The negative always presupposes the positive, without which there would be nothing to negate. This great principle is also the case here. In the centre of the organism of the five events is the new, most positive, light-filled Christ Event, even though it is accompanied by a sorathic shadow. This event forms the mirror axis between the first two and the last events and thereby links them, forming an actual organism: in the Ahriman Event something of the Michael impulse is reflected, even if in a contrary manner. In the Sorath Event, something of the ending of Kali Yuga lights up, though again in a contrary fashion. The situation is actually as follows: first the Michael and the Ahriman Events have in common the fact that they both relate — with reversed symptoms — to the human connection to intellectuality and spirituality. Secondly, The Age of Light, as the epoch after the end of Kali Yuga can also be called, and the Sorath Event relate to the possibility of a far-reaching spiritual *enlightenment* or spiritual *darkening*.

In order to be able to understand the organic character of these initial five events of the Age of Michael more thoroughly, we must turn to consider more closely the *tasks* which faced mankind in the occurrence of each event.

Let us therefore consider the five events from the point of view of the tasks they set us, which were, and still are, to be fulfilled in the first third of the Age of Michael.

1. The Spiritualization of Thinking

The fundamental task of the Age of Michael which began in 1879 was often described by Rudolf Steiner with a single phrase — 'the spiritualization of the intellect' — or with words that circumscribed this phrase.[21] On 18 July 1924 in Arnhem he characterized the task of Michael as follows:

> He administers that which is indeed spiritual but which culminates in human intellectual conceptions. Michael is not the spirit who nourishes and fosters intellectuality; but everything that he gives as spirituality wants to light up in human beings in the form of ideas, in the form of thoughts — in the form of ideas and thoughts that grasp what is spiritual. Michael wants the human being to be a free being who in his concepts and ideas sees what comes to him as revelation from spiritual worlds.

By the spiritualization of the intellect fostered by Michael is meant that human understanding, which has developed and practised a certain mastery through natural scientific training, now has the task to empower itself in the sphere of the spiritual, something which in previous times was reserved to *faith*. The split between faith in spiritual realities and knowledge of what is only sense-perceptible is to be overcome through this; natural science is to be complemented and extended by a *science of the spirit*. When Rudolf Steiner characterized anthroposophy or spiritual science as an inspiration from Michael, then in Steiner's inaugural deed it can be seen that such a science was created, with all its foundations and with countless particular research results; in it can be seen a pioneering fulfilment of the very first task which the Age of Michael places before mankind.

Already at the outset of his work within the Theosophical Society, Steiner confirmed in a letter, to those who were then comrades and then later opponents of Wilhelm Hübbe-Schleiden, his own words as those which indicated the right way forward: 'This path into the realm of the spirit today leads through the realm of the intellect.'[22]

Thinking must therefore become capable of thinking with the same exactitude as has become normal in thinking about the natural world of the senses.

Word-free thinking

Intimately connected to this main task is the requirement that this thinking free itself from what is bound up with words. This is actually a basic condition for finding the way to Michael at all. After the Christmas Conference (December 1923) Rudolf Steiner once said about this:

> The most energetic spiritual struggle is in fact going on today in this direction, because it is very much the case among a large proportion of mankind today that it is not thinking that is going on but thinking in words. But thinking in words is no way to Michael. One comes to Michael only when one passes right through words; one comes to spiritual experiences when one does not depend on words. [...] *This is in fact the secret of modern initiation: to get beyond words to the experience of the spiritual.* This is not to offend against the feeling for the beauty of language. For precisely when one no longer thinks in language does one begin to feel it and to have it streaming as an element of feeling in itself and from itself. But that is something for which the human being must strive for today.[23]

For thinking to pass beyond language into the realm of the concrete-spiritual — the core text with which one can work on this double Michaelic challenge is Steiner's *Philosophie der Freiheit* (the English title is: *The Philosophy of Freedom* or *The Philosophy of Spiritual Activity*). Already in the fourth chapter it draws attention to the difference between words, concepts and thinking. The reader who works with the book is led to an ever more differentiated distinction of this threefoldness.

The Experience of the Arché of Thought

On the path of *The Philosophy of Spiritual Activity*, the patient student will himself finally achieve knowledge of the objectively real spiritual being of thinking. Steiner describes this being in the final chapter of the book as the primal being (*Urwesen*) that all human beings grasp as common to them all when they become active in thinking. To the question of W.J. Stein as to whether this primal being was a real spiritual being, Steiner replied: 'It is a kind of group soul of mankind, it is the eldest of the Archai who is on the way to becoming a Spirit of Form.'[24] An indication of the most far-reaching importance! While all other group souls are to be transcended in the Age of Michael, the Spirit of Thought that appears in the free activity of thinking is in the most modern sense the Spirit that unites human beings and creates community! A Michaelic community is really not at all conceivable without this real Spirit of Thought who is called on through the free activity of thinking. In this sense, Michael communities must be first and foremost communities of thought and knowledge.

Feelings and free deeds can and should connect to the accomplishments of common efforts in thinking. A real 'harmony of feelings' that is in tune with the times can, however, only be based on truth or wisdom that is experienced in common.

The Spirit of Thinking in Words

The two Michael tasks — to reach beyond language through thinking, and through thinking to come to the spirit, whereby on the path of *The Philosophy of Spiritual Activity* the Spirit of Thinking itself has first to be cognized — are denied by that other spirit which is closely related to human intellect and which works in opposition to these two tasks. Ahriman-Mephisto seeks to keep the human being bound to the word. With grandiose cynicism he teaches the pupil in Goethe's *Faust* about the alleged superiority of the word over all concepts: 'for even where concepts are lacking, a word comes to hand at the right time' — this is the radical counter-teaching to the Michaelic task of freeing oneself from words. Ahriman thereby shows himself very concretely to be the actual opponent both of the Spirit of Thinking and of the Archangel Michael, and who must be thought of as standing in a close relationship with the latter. When Michael calls on human beings to bring to the spiritual realm from which it originally stems an intellect that is free of words, Ahriman seeks to tear the intellect away from the spirit and verbalize it — that is, to subject itself to ever-newer, more brilliant, professional, and other kinds of expression, and to lose itself in these. The philosophy of the twentieth century which ignored Steiner's timely work in the field of cognition has thus to a great extent, and with a tragic necessity, become a mirror of this mephisto-phelian bondage of thinking to language; 'thinking in words' has not only remained a general human phenomenon but, as it were, a doctrine of professional philosophy which has also taken hold of medical research. A further fall of thinking was rendered inevitable by this: thinking was held to originate only in the brain or in the genes.

The Philosophy of Spiritual Activity is therefore really the actual Michael-work of Steiner, naturally not only because, as previously mentioned, it is the only one of his works to be mentioned in Steiner's considerations of Michael in his *Anthroposophical Leading Thoughts*, but rather, for the factual reasons adduced in the foregoing discussion. It is not a question of whether or not the name or *the word* Michael appears in that book (*The Philosophy...*) or not. Its inner substance fulfils the most fundamental requirements of the new Michael age.

It may have already become apparent that the actual fulfilment of the first spiritual task which Michael had begun to set in 1879 must be of the greatest importance for the fulfilment of all the subsequent tasks of the present age, especially the fifth, the Ahriman Event.

2. The New Clairvoyance

The end of the Age of Darkness (Kali Yuga) introduced a new age in which, after the necessary darkening of the spirit, the whole of mankind will again become clairvoyant — an epoch to which there is no visible end.

However, this clairvoyance should be based on the fulfilment of the *first* fundamental task—that is, on the spiritualization of thinking. Just as an abstract, sense-free thinking represents the end of the *old* clairvoyance and, as it were, the most recent evolutionary product of the metamorphosis of that clairvoyance, so it was also to become the starting point for the new clairvoyance which began after 1899.[25]

That can only happen when thinking is *spiritualized* in the aforementioned sense. If this does not occur, the result is clairvoyance of one kind or another which lacks a basis in thinking. It is vital in the case of the task set by the second event that it be accomplished on the basis of the fulfilment of the first task. At the present time it is quite clear that many people have clairvoyant experiences but in a form which lacks any cognitive basis, and which then easily becomes affected by subjectivity and error. For this reason, Steiner constantly emphasized the importance of a striving to educate oneself in thinking, which is already assured by the serious study of spiritual science. He once emphasized that the greatest opposition today is not between materialists and spiritualists but between people who want to gain access to the spirit in *comfortable* ways and those who are prepared to make strenuous efforts in spiritual thinking in order to achieve it.[26]

The Functions of the Lotus Flowers (Chakras)

In earlier epochs of human development a number of astral sense organs were active. They were and are called lotus flowers or chakras.

When the human being was still in the condition of a dreamy, dull consciousness, these organs were active within him naturally, by themselves. As consciousness awoke in the course of development, the organs darkened, and their activity ceased. The beginning of the Age of Light (1900) stimulated the chakras into activity again, but the human being today must himself contribute something to the development of these spiritual sense organs.

There are altogether seven such organs: the four-petalled, the six-petalled, the ten-petalled,[27] the twelve-petalled, the sixteen-petalled, the two-petalled, and the thousand-petalled lotus flowers. They lie near to corresponding physical organs or organic areas — the four-petalled in the sexual region, the thousand-petalled at the crown of the head, and the five others between these two. A good overview of the seven astral sense organs and their relation to the physical body, on the one hand, and to the forces of the seven planets, from the Moon to Saturn, on the other, is provided by Werner Bohm in his book *Die Lotusblumenkraft*[28] (The Power of the Lotus Flowers), for which the anthroposopher Hans Hasso von Veltheim wrote the introduction.

In order to develop the lotus flowers in a way *that is in tune with modern times*, very specific conscious exercises must be carried out. Such exercises are given in Rudolf Steiner's book for spiritual training, *Knowledge of the Higher Worlds, How Is It Achieved?* These have the effect that half of the total functions of each astral sense organ are exercised; the functions that had already been active then become newly active by themselves, and the whole lotus flower turns in the correct direction, which today means to the right.

The first and seventh lotus flowers are not *directly* activated by a modern schooling. Today the emphasis is first on the two-petalled (in the region between the eyebrows); then the sixteen-petalled (in the larynx area) and the twelve-petalled (the heart chakra).

The sixteen-petalled lotus flower in the larynx area can serve as an example. Through the systematic practice of *eight* exercises, the whole lotus flower is activated in an appropriate manner. Without such an active awakening of the named functions by these eight very specific inner exercises, the lotus flower can indeed again become active after the end of Kali Yuga — through mediumistic practices or 'by itself', but it will then only function inadequately and will turn in the wrong direction which, according to Steiner, must bring about distorted insights into the spiritual world.

The Two-petalled Lotus Flower

The most important lotus flower in a certain sense for a *modern*, new clairvoyance is the two-petalled chakra between the eyes. Bohm associates this with Jupiter. It is the organ of clairvoyance which is already prevalent in sense-free thinking. This is the organ which Krishna—in a world-historical premiere, so to speak— awakened in his pupil Arjuna, and which allowed Arjuna a view of the world of *pure thought and its laws*; first into the law of reincarnation and that of the immortality of the human spirit. Here there is only one thing to practise: sense-free thinking itself. This happens today already simply through earnest study of spiritual scientific writings. The achievement of the first task of the Michael Age therefore has to do with the activation of the functions of *this* lotus flower. The spiritualization of thinking which was described as the first task therefore forms at the same time the very best basis for the activation of all the other lotus flowers.

From analytical thought to formative thinking

Spiritualized thinking overcomes the merely dissecting, analytical thinking which rules in the natural scientific way of thinking, but also indirectly in today's 'spiritual sciences'. This spiritualized thinking alone can receive the new spiritual wave which has been flowing into humankind since 1879/1899 in adequate ways. Rudolf Steiner spoke of this in a New Year lecture on 1 January 1919 (GA 187):

There are [...] two ways of forming thoughts. One way is the analytical, which [...] plays such a prominent role in natural science today. When someone says something today, one nails him to strict definitions. But strict definitions are nothing more than distinctions between things, which one defines. This way of thinking is a kind of mask which especially serves those spirits which would like to tear us apart and which are present in this struggle [i.e. this war—tr.] [...]. One must clearly distinguish this way of thinking, to which those various powers have access that seek to tear men apart, from the other, which is the only one employed by spiritual science. It is a completely different form of conception, a completely different way of thinking. It is, unlike the analytical approach, a *shaping, formative* way of thinking. [...] When you think in an analytical way, when you think like a natural scientist thinks today, then you think just like certain spirits of the ahrimanic world, and these ahrimanic spirits can therefore penetrate into your soul. When you take the *shaping, formative* path of thinking, however, metamorphosed thinking—I could even say Goethean thinking—as is represented, for example, in the forms of our columns and capitals [those in the Goetheanum Building—*tr.*] and so on; when you take this path of formative thinking, to which attention is also given in all the books that I have tried to place into spiritual science, this thinking is intimately connected to the human being. Only those beings are capable of working in this formative way, in the way the human being works with his thinking in himself, who are related to normal human evolution.

[...] when you allow yourself to think in this formative way through spiritual science [...] you can never come on to a false path. People today only need to hold to this spiritual scientific way of thinking, then they cannot be harmed by those demonic beings who are rolling in with the new wave of the Spirits of Personality as accompanying phenomena.

If we are called through the event of 1879 to spiritualize our thinking and to direct it to the supersensible and the spiritual, then in this thinking the old, dissecting analytical thinking cannot be one-sidedly maintained; thinking should become a *formative* process in the sense indicated.

The great tasks posed by the events of 1879 and 1899 also include moving over to thinking in metamorphoses, to mobile holistic thinking. The new formative thinking is a gift or, rather, a task of the new spiritual wave which began to stream into mankind in the years mentioned. Without such a thinking it will hardly be possible to deal with the task posed by the third spiritual event of the Michael Age.

3. The New Understanding of Christ and the Knowledge of the Etheric

The appearance of Christ in the Etheric places before mankind the task of a purely spiritual experience and understanding of

Christ, free of all sense-perceptible facts, oral communications, or documents. The fulfilment of *this* task too depends to a certain extent on the fulfilment of the previous two: only a clairvoyance based on spiritualized thinking can lead to a *sure* experience of the new appearance of Christ. It could be objected that in Rudolf Steiner's first mystery drama, *The Portal of Initiation*, the Etheric Christ Event is foreseen not by the spiritual teacher Benedictus but by the 'naive seer' Theodora, but that only shows that a clairvoyant untrained in thinking can also see what is right and very important when he or she possesses pure and selfless mores to a high degree, a precondition that applies to Theodora. And yet it is precisely she who, in this sense of pure seeing, later finds herself unable to protect herself from an intrigue by Lucifer which is spun in the third drama, *The Guardian of the Threshold*. Unable to see through it, she falls an innocent victim.

The Understanding of Etheric Space

To the *preconditions* for a new understanding of Christ belong spiritual scientific thoughts about the nature of the etheric realm in which the essential was not the point but *the periphery*.

With regard to the year 1933 which Rudolf Steiner indicated as the beginning of the etheric appearance of Christ, a pupil of Steiner's had a book published in the same year which presented the fundamental principles of the etheric realm: this was the small essay *Physical and Ethereal Spaces* by George Adams. It forms a good foundation from which to overcome all one-sided, spatial, centric thinking and ideas. While Christ appeared at the Turning Point of Time at a particular point in Palestine in the northern hemisphere of the planet, His etheric appearance in the twentieth century was bound to no particular place as a *centre* for His activity. The 'place of His activity' is the entire world-spanning etheric *periphery*. The reality of the etheric activity of Christ cannot be adequately grasped with a thinking that remains one-sidedly physically centred.

How difficult it can be even for christologically oriented

people to think in a concrete etheric-spatial way shows itself in how difficult it is to harmonize Christian festivals in the northern hemisphere with the seasonal realities in the southern hemisphere, as Rudolf Steiner had urged should be done.[29] The Christian festivals were fixed for the physical northern hemisphere; in the future they must be brought into harmony with the etheric realities of the entire globe.

Rudolf Steiner's *Soul Calendar*, created in 1912, can also lead to an *experience* of the etheric. The 52 weekly verses are arranged in such a way that each verse for the northern hemisphere corresponds to one for the southern hemisphere. One who works with the calendar can thereby live into the etheric realm, which encompasses both hemispheres of our planet in which the new activity of the Christ has been effective since 1933.

Christ Experiences in a Darkened Age

It may seem as if this third and central event within the organism of the five was the least evident of the five, the one that remained the most unknown due to the parallel appearance of National Socialism and the Second World War, and also due to the ongoing effects of Bolshevism. All the more remarkable is it, then, that precisely during the darkness of the years of the Nazi genocide, some souls attained an experience of Christ during their lives or after death. An example of the latter is found in the book *Eine Weile im Blumenreich*[30] [A Time in the Realm of Flowers], in which such an experience is described in a naive-poetic form. The Swede Barbro Karlén (b. 1954) wrote this book when she was twelve years old, in Sweden, which had been the land where in January 1910 Rudolf Steiner had first announced the Etheric Christ Event to mankind.

The Christ Event of the young Swede was not the only one there. In a book published by two other Swedes, *Sie erlebten Christus*[31] [They Experienced Christ], can be found numerous other notable accounts of such experiences. And certainly there will have been other, as yet unreported experiences of this kind, and no doubt there will be more in the future.

However, such experiences were and are gifts of grace, most of them after unimaginable suffering.

A Spiritual Understanding of the Gospels

Something else that belongs to a free, conscious perception of the Christ Event, alongside knowledge of the nature of the etheric realm, is a spiritual understanding of the Gospels. Rudolf Steiner expressly referred to this in Sweden in January 1910 on the occasion of his first communications about the new Christ Event: 'Around 1933 the Gospels must be so well-understood in their spiritual sense', he said, according to notes made by Marie von Sivers, 'that they will have worked to prepare the way for the Christ. Otherwise, endless confusion of the soul would result.'

At the beginning of 1910, Steiner gave spiritual scientific lecture cycles on the Gospels of St Luke and St John; the Berne cycle on the Gospel of St Matthew followed in September, and in 1912, finally, the cycle on the Gospel of St Mark—to name only the most notable of Steiner's lectures on this subject. In October 1913, shortly after the laying of the Foundation Stone of the First Goetheanum, Steiner began his lectures on the *Fifth Gospel*, in which he spoke about completely new results of his spiritual research, about which there is nothing to be found in the four Gospels. Interestingly, these revelations were also made in Scandinavia, in Oslo.

Steiner's Gospel cycles had therefore created the preconditions, named by him in 1910, for the fulfilment of the 'Christ-Task', and numerous people had taken these spiritual scientific thoughts into their own thinking and feeling. And yet in 1933 there *was* 'endless confusion'! The 'preparation for the Christ' achieved by a relatively small number of people had, seen in terms of mankind as a whole, evidently not been enough.

However, we can also learn from the notes of those Stockholm lectures that mankind still has about 2,500 years in which to fulfil this task. That is a bit longer than it took for a spiritual scientific understanding of the first Christ Event to become possible.

The new Christ Event will unfold over long periods of time

into the future and will only be deeply understood in stages. As it was accompanied at the time of its first appearance by the Sorath shadow, this being too must be taken into consideration.

The Encounter with the Beast from the Abyss

At this point a statement must be mentioned which Rudolf Steiner made on 20 September 1924 during his lectures on the Apocalypse: 'One would have to say in the sense of the Apocalyptist: *Before the Etheric Christ can be comprehended in the right way, mankind must first have passed through the confrontation with the Beast which will rise in 1933.'*[32]

From 1998 onwards this urging no longer sounded from the already fatally effective shadow but from concrete world-historical reality: from that year onwards, passing through the confrontation with Sorath has become *the* precondition for the right comprehension of the Etheric Christ. But what does 'passing through' mean in this case? It can only be a matter of bringing the highest possible cognitional perspectives to bear on the encounter with the Beast. The origin and meaning of evil in evolution—that is the further question which must be answered in order to arrive at a correct understanding of the Etheric Christ, at least in an elementary sense. Let us therefore turn to the fifth event and the deep task of knowledge that is bound up with it.

4. The Opponent of Christ and the Knowledge of Absolute Goodness

Sorath is *the* cosmic opponent of Christ. To comprehend his activity requires a radical understanding of the function of evil in evolution. Where does evil originate? From the eternal? Is it in 'eternal' confrontation with the good? In view of the radical evil that shows itself in Sorath's activity, such questions must be posed and answered.

All evil originates in a higher good. In spiritual scientific terms: from the region of the Cherubim and Seraphim. A number of these high beings in times very far in past evolution refused the sacrifices that were brought to them by the Thrones. Through

this they became conscious of their own eternity. Simultaneously, through the Thrones' act of sacrifice, the evolutionary
factor of *Time* came into being. Through their denial of the
sacrifice, on the other hand, the Cherubim and Seraphim called
into the now ongoing temporal evolution beings which could
seize control of the sacrificial substance that did not have any
special purpose for them. *This was the moment of the birth of Time,
as well as the moment of the birth of the opposition of certain beings
against those high beings who had first brought about this opposition.*[33]

On the Cosmic plane all is good

Rudolf Steiner once discussed these matters at the end of a lecture on the threefold nature of evil in March 1909: 'Everything on
the cosmic plane is good, and evil only has its existence for a
certain time. Therefore those who believe in the eternity of evil
confuse the temporal with the eternal, and so one can only
comprehend evil if one rises from the temporal to the eternal.'[34]

These words outline the task of knowledge which has to be
fulfilled here. It can only be fulfilled when again, a clear distinction is made between the temporal and the eternal. This
distinction was blurred for centuries by the Eighth Council of
Constantinople (869–70), in that the Council denied that the
human being has an independent spirit, and dogmatically
degraded the image of man to that of a mere being with a soul
that has a few spiritual characteristics. The Council of 869 robbed
mankind of its spiritual consciousness. It is no accident that it
took place under the inspiration of *Sorath*, as Steiner stated in
1918.[35]

Only a new spiritual consciousness can lead to a concrete
experience of the eternal, just as soul consciousness must
experience itself as immersed in *time*. Then the cosmic plane
borne by the Cherubim and Seraphim reveals itself to be the
sphere of the eternally good, which knows no opposition or
'competitors'. The dualism between good and evil, or indeed any
other kind of dualism, has no place here. Here only the great
absolute Good rules, while everything good that stands in

opposition to something evil may only be called a 'lesser', relative and limited good. For the 'lesser good' experiences its limits precisely in that evil! Evil, by contrast, finds its own limits in what is eternal, out of which evil itself first emerged. The concept of an 'eternal evil' is as absurd as that of a wooden iron. It is the nature of evil to be temporal and to remain in need of *higher values* which authorize its activity. Only through such knowledge can three dangers be avoided in the confrontation with evil: the fear of evil, the hatred of evil, and the false fascination with evil.

Christ as the Image of the Cherubim

The facts outlined above were presented by Rudolf Steiner in a more profound manner in his lecture cycle *Die Evolution vom Gesichtspunkte des Wahrhaftigen* [Evolution from the Perspective of Truthfulness] (GA 132). He shows in this cycle that the Christ Being descended from that high region of the cosmic plane where the Cherubim and Seraphim rule. And just as those high Beings could have avoided the emergence of evil, so Christ could have avoided taking Judas into his circle and could have avoided being betrayed by him. The relation of Christ to Judas corresponds to that of the Cherubim and Seraphim towards the evil that was induced into evolution by them. This fact lies at the root of the artistic intention pursued by Leonardo da Vinci in his painting of the *Last Supper*. His unconscious spiritual intention caused him to paint that moment in the Last Supper when Christ, out of love for the evolution of mankind, Himself gives leave in full freedom for evil to do its work.

Leonardo intuited the connection between freedom and love on the one hand, and the necessary prevalence of evil in the temporal world on the other — this is what gives to his painting its spiritual, world-historical significance.

Goethe too knew of the mystery of absolute good in relation to relative evil, which is only allowed and enabled to act with the permission of a higher good. He presented this truth in the Prologue to his *Faust*. It is the Lord God who *allows* Mephisto to attack Faust. Goethe knew also that without the 'seasoning', the stimulation provided by evil, the human being all too easily 'falls asleep' in his striving for the higher good.

Goethe's image of Judas is also to be found among Steiner's later investigations; Goethe does not at all regard Judas as the trivial traitor he is often held to be; rather, he sees him as a man who strove for the good but in the *wrong* way. Judas hoped through his deed to be able to urge Christ to reveal His power and glory, as it were, once and for all.[36]

The Star of Judas

The betrayal that was necessary for the realization of the Mystery of Golgotha made Judas into one who had a deep knowledge of the mystery of evil, to which his two following incarnations as St Augustine and Leonardo da Vinci increasingly bear witness. No-one can understand the deeper aspects of Leonardo's *Last Supper* who does not know that it had been the deed of betrayal and its spiritual execution which enabled the artist to represent that moment in which Christ, in full freedom, called forth the violence of evil against Himself by dipping the morsel of bread into Judas' bowl.

It is a remarkable fact that just around the time of Sorath's sharpest attack yet, a fragmentary early Christian text, the *Gospel of Judas*, was rediscovered and made public, from which we learn that Judas too had his 'eternal star', and was taught by Christ to follow it.[37]

Beyond Polarities

We must in our thoughts and feelings first seek to reach up to the highest possible good in order to comprehend evil. It originates in the highest region of the spirit in which 'all is good' — that is, good in the sense of an absence of contraries. Steiner already posited such a supra-dualistic starting point in his *Philosophy of Spiritual Activity*: he did not proceed from any kind of opposites (I vs the world, subject vs object, good vs evil, spirit vs matter etc.) but from thinking, which precedes all these dualities and encompasses all of them.

We are accustomed, even chained, to the world of opposites in our thinking and feeling today so that rising to such a perspective beyond them may perhaps even seem impossible to many. But it must be attempted. Every wandering in the heights may lead through dangerous terrain, and one's vision may be obscured by mist at times; but just as there is an upper limit to all mist and clouds, so there is also, above, a limit to evil.

'In the spirit is harmony', Steiner once formulated as the daily verse for Friday.[38]

Where there is no harmony; where opposition and war rule in private or public life, the spirit has not become determinant. To fathom the deep truth of this supra-dualistic daily verse belongs to the task which has to be fulfilled to a considerable extent precisely at this Sorath point in the Age of Michael. Did Richard Wagner not sense something of this sphere beyond all polarities when he wrote the libretto for his 'Good *Friday* Magic', and then composed the music?

The St Anthony of the Isenheim Altar

Matthias Grünewald too knew of the 'harmony in the spirit': his painting of St Anthony not only shows the truly appalling demons before whom St Anthony appears to be utterly defenceless, but also shows the ardent seeker holding firmly *to one thing*, to the rosary in his hands, the sign of his trust in God. Even in that dark hour in which he believes that he has been abandoned by God, he does not allow his faith to be wrested from him.

Above the dramatic scene in the lower and middle panels of the painting reign, in majestic calm, mountain peaks bedecked with ice and snow, and above them the face of God the Father is visible. This sublime spiritual world rays down to the world below and borders on the soul world in which the temptations of St Anthony are taking place. On the border of both worlds is a devilish figure in a vain struggle against St Michael, who stands above him wielding a much longer spear.

To the right of the crucifixion panel stands the same St

Anthony, but many years after the temptation shown; a dignified old man, calm and composed with a rod-shaped Tau Cross in his left hand. Behind and a little above him is a horned demon who has broken through a window and who now releases his stinking hissing breath into the soul space in which St Anthony is placed. From his own long experience, the saint knows about the machinations of the demonic world. He is not disturbed by their efforts which are allowed by a higher authority, at least he is *no longer* disturbed. His many glimpses into the realm of the eternal, which he has gained through his repeated experience of life's troubles, have brought him an unshakable inner calm.

The Perspective of the Sorcerer's Apprentice

In his famous ballad, Goethe takes up a theme which he found in Lucian of Samosata. The sorcerer's apprentice can no longer cope with the forces he has let loose, and falls into a panic. A mighty, uncontrollable evil appears. This corresponds to many people's shared erroneous beliefs in an evil that competes with the good, and is perhaps even able to overcome it. The powerless sorcerer's apprentice's perspective of evil can only be overcome by looking up to the eternal powers of the cosmic plane. In Goethe's ballad they appear in the form of the old lord and master, who is able to restore order with a few magic words:

> Broomstick! Broomstick!
> Into the corner, go!
> As spirits you must know
> That you are only called to serve
> The will of this old master.

The Two Races

Rudolf Steiner raised such artistically formed inspirations by Leonardo, Grünewald, or Goethe into the light of full knowledge. He showed how all evil must be seen in the light of a higher good, and he showed how it is precisely in the struggle to understand evil that a higher good can and must be created by human beings themselves. This higher good created by human beings will be the Manichaean ferment in the development of the sixth great Earth Period. This period will begin after the end of the fifth Earth Period at the end of the seventh post-Atlantean Epoch. Then that time of development will begin in which those belonging to the good or spiritual 'race' will do all they can to bring as many out of the unspiritual race as possible on to another path of development. A true Manichaeism is unthinkable without knowledge of absolute Good as the origin of all evil. Only evil that stems from the higher good can be led back to the good. This struggle to *redeem* evil will only ultimately be decided in the very distant future: in the *sixth* cultural epoch of the *sixth* epoch of the *sixth* Great Period (i.e. the Venus Period) of the entire process of evolution of our solar system. This perspective is also one of the ways of interpreting the number 666.

The task which is therefore placed at 'the Sorath point' of the fifth event of the current Age of Michael aims at the knowledge of the highest unlimited good, and is to free the human being finally from the 'error of the number two', in which he is caught as long as he knows only a lesser good which is confronted by a supposedly all-powerful evil.

9/11 and the Gondishapur of our time

This error of dualism, which all higher harmony negates, was evident not only in the fact that the human being was reduced from a threefold to a twofold being (body and soul) by the church dogma of 869; it shows itself also in this present Sorath time in the inclination to divide human beings into absolute good and evil. It therefore has to do with a perverse projection of what is *actually* absolute into the temporal realm. The slogan of 'the axis of evil' and of the 'axis of good' that is posited contrary to it shows from which spirit stem those power brokers who, as the string-pullers or accomplices, have been responsible for the greatest crime in recent human history — the attacks of 11 September 2001. With its infernal use of torture, which was made to seem justified by the 'War On Terror' and which represents a renaissance of the tortures inflicted on the Templars, 9/11 was a sorathic prelude to the actual 'Gondishapur'-activity in our time today. This activity is ultimately directed against all spiritual knowledge.

The sorathic battle against the pure form of spiritual science

While the Academy of Gondishapur soaked up Aristotelian knowledge and developed it in an un-Christian direction, something very similar is going on at present with the spiritual science of Rudolf Steiner. Its actual spiritual character is to be stripped away, intellectualized, 'contextualized', computerized, and cannibalized for certain particular interests, and thereby its actual substance will be annihilated. The Gondishapur of the first post-Christian era lay within the territory of today's SW Iran; the present 'Gondishapur' embraces the region from Silicon Valley to Salt Lake City, a region which extends its electro-magnetic intellectual tentacles via the Internet and Facebook throughout the entire world. The point here is not to criticize the human instruments involved in such efforts. One who wishes to understand a 'Reinecke' has to look towards his inspirer, as Steiner's fourth Mystery Drama shows. It would not, for example, be worth discussing the fact that an astonishingly well-'informed' personality (a Ph.D.) is today seeking to become a leading 'standard-setting' specialist in Anthroposophy; he happens to be from the world of Mormonism, which, amongst other things, teaches the physical return of Christ and which, without being requested to do so, provides for humanity the blessings of 'salvation-bestowing' post-mortem baptisms (one such was performed on 'Rudolf Steiner', on 20 January 1992). Statements such as the following suffice to suggest the intellectual and moral standing of the personality in question: 'If Anthroposophists really want to know whether Steiner was a Plato or a Cagliostro, they must release him from the prison of their own interpretations.'[39]

Who could take seriously someone capable of such a comment, who mocks in this way both the karmic realities linked to Steiner as well as healthy human reason? — to say nothing of other things.

It is noteworthy in the fullest sense of the word, however, how many 'well-known' anthroposophers with a certain, scarcely restrained inclination to hanker after recognition by the world of academia turn a blind eye to the tendentious one-sidednesses, absurdities, and distastefulness of this enterprise.

This shows a notable clouding of the capacity for judgement. The source of this clouding lies in the spiritual beings under discussion here and in their following; spiritual science could teach people to identify this source, but apparently, not all 'anthroposophers' seek what is vital spiritual scientific knowledge.

Why a pure form of spiritual science is necessary

One who really sought anthroposophy with all the force of his thinking and heart, and who therefore had no illusions about the growing spiritual opposition to spiritual science, especially in the West, was perhaps the most important and far-seeing pupil of Steiner in the West: D.N. Dunlop (1868–1935). Immediately after Steiner's death Dunlop said something that is truly eye-opening in today's context and which could drive away all the fog that befuddles discernment. He said:

> Ahriman knows the strength of his weapons; he knows the stupe-faction which the senses have brought about in the spiritual life of man; he works consciously in the fear men have in face of concrete spiritual revelation. We should realize that the opposition to Spiritual Science is only just beginning; it will grow stronger and *more insidious ... Therefore for us there must be no compromise with materialism in whatever form it may be; we have to assert a wisdom that is 'not of this world' and therefore in its pure form,* inaccessible to the darts of Ahriman.[40]

This devious, obstructive opposition is hard at work. In this sense, Sorath, who in a certain sense can be regarded as a 'John the Baptist' for Ahriman, has already made straight the ways for his master, Ahriman.

Darkness surrounding earlier incarnations

The attacks of 9/11 and the coercive political measures at home and abroad associated with the event were merely the catastrophic prelude to the sorathic attempt to sweep away *everything* of a positive nature that has begun to flourish, if not to blossom, since the beginning of the Age of Michael: through a fear of terror spread throughout the world, humanity was to be thrown into a total loss of spirit and into money-obsessed materialism. Again, in the Apocalypse lectures to the priests, Steiner gave an incisive diagnosis of what would happen if mankind was *not* ready for the encounter with the Beast. On 22 September 1924, Steiner said:

> Otherwise nothing else can happen than that one day in the future everything human beings have experienced since the year 666 will be torn from them, everything they will already have experienced under the influence of the developing individuality. Darkness would spread over all the earlier incarnations of humanity, and a different world evolution would take the place of the evolution of the Earth. We can already see the beginnings of this today; all human weaknesses will be used, especially people's vanity and their lack of truthfulness, to bring people over to the wrong side.[41]

*

This fourth event, the activity of the opponent of Christ at the present time, brought, and is also bringing again, the test of how far the previous events and their tasks have been understood and fulfilled. With regard to the most recent events of our time, this test can only be withstood if the events around 11 September 2001 and the tissue of lies with which they were immediately surrounded, and also the more recent obstructive, and, from all those playing the 'Reinecke' role today, mostly unconscious opposition to R. Steiner's work are all observed and contemplated with spiritual thoughts (which also include the 'thought' of a Sun Demon), and if these thoughts can then rise to grasp the highest, absolute goodness in world evolution. This absolute goodness originates in a region in which absolute truth and absolute beauty prevail. From there, Christ descended to Palestine at the Turning Point of Time. Since then He has begun to guide the human being who turns to Him in freedom once more, up towards this high realm of spirit which is also the true home of the actual human I itself.

The preparation for the encounter with the Beast consists, therefore, first in an honest acknowledgment of all possible weakness, vanity, and untruthfulness, and then, to emphasize it once more, in an energetic, clear-thinking cognition of the eternally good. If both of these are striven for in an honest manner then 'the Etheric Christ too can be comprehended by man in the right way'.

Thus the fulfilment of the task set by the fourth event can lead to a deep reception of the fruits of the *third* and central event of our Michaelic age, the event which will last long into the future.

5. Knowledge of Ahriman—the Test of the Sword of Michael

If the fourth event and the task connected to it—of the knowledge of absolute good—are slept through, then the fifth event— the incarnation of Ahriman—will turn out to be all the more damaging for mankind.

As already mentioned, this fifth event comes soon after the fourth—'before even a part of the third millennium . . . has run its course'. Ahriman will seek to harvest what his 'herald' has sown. He can only be confronted where there has been a 'harvest' by *human beings* from the first four events. The incarnation of Ahriman represents in a certain respect the greatest test in the first half of this current Age of Michael. The task consists in forging a spiritualized thinking into a spiritual sword, before which the arts of Ahriman must fail.

Like the ahrimanic Sun Demon Sorath, Ahriman seeks especially to obliterate all human knowledge of karma. In the eleventh scene of the second Mystery Drama *The Soul's Probation*, he appears to Maria with this intention; she wants to work meditatively on her great and detailed review (*Rückschau*) of the Middle Ages. In complete harmony with the origin of all evil in the Good (see the earlier discussion relating to the fourth task), she says:

The high powers of destiny have wisely
chosen you as the adversary;
for you further everything you seek to hinder.

But she also knows:

There is only one place in the land of spirits
where that sword can be forged,
the sight of which makes you withdraw.
It is that realm in which the souls of men
form knowledge from powers of reason
and then transform into spirit wisdom.

Maria speaks here of the sword of spiritualized thinking. The
spiritual teacher Benedictus has to grasp this sword in the last
scene of the drama *The Soul's Awakening* in order to recognize
Ahriman and to be able to drive him from the field. When
Benedictus directs his gaze of recognition at Ahriman, Ahriman
himself says:

It is time for me to quit his circle quickly,
for as soon as his vision
can *think* me as I am,
there will soon arise in his thinking of me
a part of that power which will at length destroy me.
[*Ahriman withdraws*]

A mere renewal of clairvoyance, such as began to develop after
the end of Kali Yuga, would not suffice to drive Ahriman from
the field. That is clear from the eighth scene of the third drama,
The Guardian of the Threshold, in which Hilarius and Trautmann
(Romanus) see Ahriman clairvoyantly but do not *know* who he is,
which leaves him completely unaffected, and allows him even to
deride those seeking advice in his realm. Only a spiritualized
thinking and a clairvoyance built on this basis serve to keep
Ahriman in his place. Without these two preconditions, even an
experience of Christ would not be sufficient in itself to cope with
Ahriman.

What we can learn from Ahriman

As Maria knows, Ahriman was set to his work by high spiritual powers. It would be false simply to seek to *avoid* him. Here too it is a question of *knowing*, but also of understanding that Ahriman can even be useful to human beings, in so far as they learn to place him and his forces at their service instead of the opposite, as is usually the case.

The spiritual pupil is, for example, directed that in all processes of deeper self-knowledge, a cold-blooded, *ahrimanic* view of one's own soul habits and vices can be extremely useful.[42]

Just as we can often observe others cold-bloodedly and without warmth, so we should occasionally observe ourselves in the same manner. The path inwards is paved by Lucifer and his 'virtues'; these are egocentricity and a warm, boundless self-love. On this path inwards a portion of 'ahrimanism' is especially effective in a therapeutic sense. This is also shown to us in the Mystery Dramas in a fine and liberating manner. In the third drama, *The Guardian of the Threshold*, Johannes Thomasius carries his subjective, unrecognized wishes even past the Guardian into the spiritual world, in the search for 'his' Theodora. This leads him to subjectively coloured and therefore illusionary spiritual experiences. The Guardian points him to the realm of Ahriman where 'wishes freeze'. Johannes recovers from his luciferic drunkenness, and after that is able to understand properly what he has spiritually experienced. We must learn to know Lucifer and Ahriman so that we are able to make them serve us more. Otherwise, we remain in unwilling servitude to them.

With Sorath this is not possible, not at this stage of evolution at any rate. He must be recognized and avoided. Here there can be no controlled co-operation but only the recognition of the eternally Good which has even authorized such an adversary whose activity too will, one day, but far in the future, be recognized as being 'wisely ordered'.

Ahriman and the 'new' clairvoyance

Ahriman will be the great beneficiary of everything that human beings have *not* developed during the four previous events of the Michaelic Age. Furthermore, he will bring a spiritualized thinking of sorts in words and phrases. Reckoning with the fact of the end of Kali Yuga, he will bestow a kind of clairvoyance which will lead to false insights and social disharmony. Rudolf Steiner gave a clear, vivid perspective of this on 15 November 1919: Ahriman will establish:

> a great occult school in the Western world [...] to bring to people through the most grandiose magic arts all that until then they will have had to achieve in clairvoyant knowledge only by means of the most strenuous effort, as is striven for here [i.e. within spiritual scientific work]. People would have to do nothing at all themselves [...] they would not need to trouble themselves about any spiritual striving.[43]

In other words: if the very first task is *freely* neglected, then through the incarnation of Ahriman, the evil fruits of this neglect can be 'harvested'.

That will lead, amongst other things, as already mentioned, to the reactivation of the astral organs of clairvoyance—the so-called lotus flowers—only in the parts that had been active in ancient times, instead of their full development.[44] The result will inevitably be warped insights in spiritual experiences. The mediumistic channelling so common around the world today or the comfortable 'past life regressions' show how successful the ahrimanic efforts in this direction have already been.

Five is the number of 'man', the bearer of freedom. It is also called the number of decision. The fifth event—the incarnation of Ahriman—will, not least, make it clear how far mankind has managed to fulfil *in freedom* the very first of the five tasks of our Michael Age.

A Deepened Knowledge of Christ

One element that belongs to the test that Ahriman will present to humanity will be the need to look back to the incarnation of Lucifer in ancient China and to its significance as a cultural impulse. Such a deep study of the other counter-force besides Ahriman is already called for by the fact that at the same time in which Ahriman incarnates in the West, China has at this time in history become a world power, if not *the* world power. A spiritual-scientifically informed understanding of the necessary roles of Ahriman and Lucifer in the development of the world and of mankind will lead to comprehensive understanding of the Christ that is to be achieved in no other way. It is the complete reversal of the ancient effort of the Essenes to hold both counter-forces at bay so that they would be able to rise to sublime spiritual heights 'undisturbed'. It was evident to the spiritual sight of Jesus of Nazareth on a visit to the Essene Order what this meant for human beings outside the walls of the Essenes: they would become all the more threatened by Lucifer and Ahriman. Today, especially at the point of this fifth event within the Michael Age thus far, a deeper understanding of Christ must be striven for precisely through a deeper knowledge of Ahriman and Lucifer, which also casts a new light on the new Christ Deed from the 1930s of the twentieth century onwards.

The Ahrimanic Resistance to the Christening of the Nature of Money

Finally, a new understanding of the role played by Judas in the Mystery of Golgotha also belongs to the tasks at this 'Ahriman point' in our epoch. In the last chapter Judas was discussed in relation to the superiority of absolute Good which *allows* evil to be. Here he must be discussed again from the viewpoint of his relationship to Ahriman–Mammon. It was after all Ahriman–Mammon who stole into Judas' soul in order to inspire him to his betrayal.

In order to facilitate a knowledge of evil, Steiner revealed 'the reversed Lord's Prayer' as the kernel of *The Fifth Gospel*. It speaks of 'bread' (and indirectly of its equivalent, 'money') 'in which it is not the will of heaven that rules' but that of Ahriman. The spiritualization of the nature of money or its Christianization — in relation to a threefolding of the social organism required by the times — was not accomplished by Christ Himself. It is not *His* task but the task of christened human beings. But just as in the fourteenth century, the strongest attack by Sorath was unleashed against just those efforts of the Templars *who were striving in this direction*, so every effort to achieve a spiritually and historically appropriate financial and economic order through a threefolding of the social organism is subject today to the most violent sorathic–ahrimanic attacks. To see through this and not to give ground to more comfortable, merely apparent solutions also belongs to the tests and tasks of the fifth event.

A first step in this direction consists of the decoupling of work and income, and in the linking of the being of money to material and non-material values that are actually produced. Both will only be able to come about in a lasting way when the illusion of a purely material world is seen through as an ahrimanic inspiration. The being of money will remain in Ahriman's power in unrecognized ways, and will only be used in egoistic or group-egoistic ways unless the human being is filled with a spirituality which is inspired by a being who serves *the whole* of mankind. In this sense the question of bread is at the same time a spiritual question; the former cannot be solved independently and separately from the latter.[45]

The Resurrected One – by Vincenzo Foppa (c.1427–1516)

Michael and Ahriman – by Charles Kovacs

Sorath — by Charles Kovacs

Head of Ahriman – by Rudolf Steiner

V. A SHORT RETROSPECTIVE OF THE FIVE EVENTS AND TASKS

From what has been outlined thus far, which obviously could be extended in several directions and rendered in more precise detail, it can be corroborated that the five named events, and the five tasks corresponding to them, have not introduced the Michael Age in any accidental sequence. And it is just as non-accidental that the first three events represent *positive* spiritual facts while the two latter provisional events have an *obstructive* spiritual content. Furthermore, the events described and their corresponding tasks form a clearly structured organism, and none of the tasks is to be fulfilled without fulfilling the others. The five tasks form the basis for tasks which the human being has to deal with during the Michaelic Age of the fifth post-Atlantean Epoch. It is also clear, as already mentioned, that the first two and the last two events occur relatively close to each other in time, while the third appears to stand more by itself. And finally, it should once more be emphasized: the last of the tasks cannot be fulfilled if the very first is not fulfilled, or at least clearly grasped. The circle of the five events and tasks is a closed one, although there will certainly be other spiritual impacts on — and tasks for — mankind in the further course of the Age of Michael.

All the five tasks characterized here in outline are tasks of *knowledge*. They are at the same time *Michael tasks*, as the events corresponding to them — with the exception of the repeated activity of Sorath with its unique rhythm of 666 years — did not occur in any of the other six archangelic ages of approximately 350 years, but exclusively in the present Michaelic Age.

Finally: *All* five tasks — and not only those relating to Sorath and Ahriman — can be regarded as *parts* of the *fundamental task* of the fifth post-Atlantean Epoch: the comprehension of evil through spiritual-scientific means.

The Factor of Freedom

In our Michael Age everything depends on the capacity for freedom. Everything depends on the cultivation of this capacity of the 'secret reality factor of the I', as the spiritual student and teacher of history Johannes Tautz used to say. This applies *above all* to the fulfilment of the very first task — the spiritualization of thinking. It is placed completely within the freedom of the human I. Rudolf Steiner's *Philosophy of Spiritual Activity* and the spiritual science developed from it, seen in the light of world history, constitute the first freely achieved fulfilment of the first of the five tasks. From the perspective of 1879 it could be said: if the task set by the event of this year is not grasped and fulfilled, then all the four following events will work out differently, and they will have to be 'fulfilled' in another way than in the Michaelic sense. And to a great extent this has been the case, to the serious detriment of the development of many individual human beings. At least then, the 'Ahriman-point' within this organism of events and tasks offers another opportunity to recognize the neglect of the first four tasks and at least to bring to them a belated fulfilment. If this opportunity too is missed, the fulfilment of the tasks set in this Michael Age will be rendered that much more difficult.

As diverse as the tasks, or the complex of tasks, set by the different events may seem, in every case their fulfilment ultimately serves — in four cases indirectly and in one case very directly — a new, truly modern knowledge of Christ, for the new Christ Event stands literally in the midst of the four other events, which are reflected in it.

VI. MICHAEL, CHRIST, SORATH AND THEIR OCCULT SIGILS

There are sigils which correspond to three of the five cosmic beings discussed in this book. The first and second sigils are, as far as we know, found only in the work of Rudolf Steiner; the third was already known to the occult traditions of Europe, for example in the writings of Agrippa von Nettesheim (1486–1535).

Let us begin with the Michael sigil, as Rudolf Steiner showed it to his pupils in his esoteric spiritual-scientific legacy, the meditative path of the School of Michael.[46]

Fig 4   The Michael Sigil (drawn by E.C. Merry)

This drawing can give us the deepest elucidation of the being and striving of Michael. The movement of this thought-filled fourfold gesture, carried out with the right arm, begins in spiritual heights and ends again in that direction. Between the two is a diving down into earthly and physical depths and through the straight-line movements a formed, clear inner soul realm.

In the language of that Michael work, *Die Philosophie der Freiheit* (*The Philosophy of Freedom*), the sigil can be experienced as follows: intuition of a free deed — that is, an action uninfluenced by physical and soul processes — is achieved in spiritual heights. This intuition is not created *by* earthly drives but in an *understanding view* of a concrete earthly deed. Before the deed is born, however, the intuition is *lovingly harboured* in the soul and immersed in individualizing moral fantasy. Only then can the idea be released to become deed. The sigil can therefore become the model of a free deed resulting from knowledge.

Whoever doubts this, or even takes the view that open discussion of this sigil, which Steiner actually first revealed only in a restricted circle, is a sacrilege, has not understood the 'signs of the times': while the new Christ Appearance set in during the 1930s of the last century, a powerful attack by the Sun Demon Sorath also began, as was described earlier. National Socialism and Bolshevism were inspired by *this* being. But in Middle Europe at least, the Anti-Christ even helped himself to the speech of the Michael sigil in order to conceal his aims and thereby to accomplish them more effectively. One only needs to visualize the blasphemous salute with the upraised outstretched arm that was made to the 'Führer' and his lunatic aims. It is the fourth part torn from the whole Michael sigil! Whoever has comprehended the connection between the archetype and the rudimentary sorathic caricature of it will see that a deeper understanding of the Michael sigil in a diagnostic, if not even in a therapeutic sense, is indispensable in order to deal with the violent Sorath attacks since the 1930s. Whoever experiences this connection will also learn to understand why so many people could be gripped by a false Michaelic enthusiasm. A remnant of the archetype was operative in the distorted caricature.

It can be seen here right into the use of gesture how different spiritual beings and their impulses engage with one another!

The Sorath Sigil

Owing to this monstrous connection between the true Michaelic image and the rudimentary sorathic counter-image, the Sorath sigil will first be given and explained in a similar way — from the speech of the sigil itself.

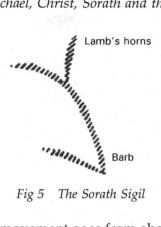

Lamb's horns

Barb

Fig 5   The Sorath Sigil

In this sigil too, the movement goes from above downwards and originates in spiritual heights. But how different the image is here! It begins not with unity but with a horned, hardened twofoldness. This alone suffices to show the onlooker that with this being it is not the *highest* spiritual realms that can rule, for to these realms, the fundamental principle applies: 'On the cosmic plane all is good', which means: harmonic unity. Twofoldness, dualism is no spiritual archetypal substance, but a product of division at some point.

The being of Sorath is at home in the delusion of the number two.[47] From this 'homeland' he works down directly into the earthly plane, immersing everything in the delusion of the number two. Let us recall that the Council of Constantinople, which did away with the threefoldness of the human being (body, soul, spirit), came about under the influence of *Sorath*. The human being was to be reduced to the Two (Dichotomy) and thus held in a continuous state of division, discord, and doubt from which he himself could no longer find the way out.

The sorathic impulse bores its way, so to speak, straight down into the now spirit-less human soul and within it—if no cognitive resistance develops there—effects a violent, sudden change of direction. This can happen in a number of ways. To cite only two examples: the denial of truth by those subjected to torture as in the case of the Templars, or, as is now taking place before our eyes today, the denial of anthroposophical truth under the influence of all kinds of vanities which cause those who have fallen into such vanities to entertain the delusion of global recognition of the spiritual science of Rudolf Steiner. In reality, this has to do with the sorathic attempt to destroy the substance of that spiritual science. This corresponds to the abrupt breakaway from the entire movement which follows the sudden, sharp change in direction mentioned above. Wherever sorathic power seeks to work, it follows this pattern: it brings about a spiritual division in human beings on earth in order suddenly to destabilize high spiritual impulses and ultimately destroy them.[48]

Rudolf Steiner spoke a number of times about the Sorath sigil, and drew it for his listeners. It appears both in his first lecture cycle on the Apocalypse in Nuremberg and also in the last such cycle, given to the priests of the Christian Community in 1924.

The Christ Sigil

Rudolf Steiner spoke about the 'sigil of the Lamb', another name he gave to the Sun Seal, as early as 1907. On 22 April 1907 he first spoke about the Sorath sigil and then about 'the sign of the Lamb'.[49] Steiner also describes it as the 'Intelligence of the Sun' and Christ as its representative. Sorath, by contrast, he describes as the Sun Demon. For 'every star has its good spirit — its Intelligence — and its evil spirit — its Demon'. Agrippa von Nettesheim already knew of this, but the sigil of the Sun Intelligence given by him differs from that given by Steiner.

The sigil of the Lamb consists of a heptagon or seven-pointed star, at each point of which stands the sign of a planet of our solar system alongside an eye, which stands for the intelligence of each planet.

Linking on to the relevant passage in the *Revelation of St John*:

This is [...] the occult sigil of the Lamb. The Lamb receives the book with the seven seals. 'And I beheld and lo, in the midst of the throne and of the four beasts, and in the midst of the elders, stood a Lamb as it had been slain, having seven horns and seven eyes, which are seven Spirits of God sent forth into all the earth.' (Revelation 5: 6) The seven points of the sigil are called 'horns'. But what do the 'eyes' signify? In occult schools the seven eyes are ascribed to the seven

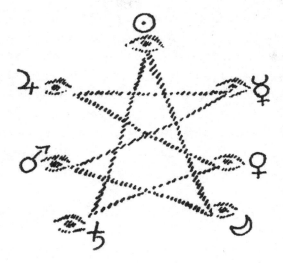

Fig 6   The Sigil of the Lamb, the Christ Sigil

planets. The seven eyes signify nothing other than the seven planets, and the names of the planets denote the spirits which are incarnated in them as their intelligences. 'Saturn' is the name of the soul of Saturn. The names of the planets are the seven planetary spirits which surround the Earth and influence human life. The Lamb, Christ, includes all seven. Christ is the Alpha and the Omega; the seven planets are related to him like the limbs to the body. The collaboration of the seven planets is wonderfully shown by the interlaced lines of the sigil. From Saturn, the line rises to the Sun, from there down to the Moon, then to Mars, Mercury and so on.

In order to experience the spiritual lines of force of this sigil inwardly, one has to proceed from 'the eye of Saturn'. 'Christ is the regent of all these cosmic bodies', said Steiner: 'they are only parts of His activity, He unites them all.' Thus all the deeds of the seven lesser [archangelic] Time Spirits, from Oriphiel to Michael, who are related to one of the seven planets, are ultimately 'parts of the activity of Christ', the cosmic co-ordinator of the temporal impulses of each of them.

A simplified form of the Christ sigil can be found in the heptagon on the third apocalyptic seal which Rudolf Steiner had painted for the Munich Whitsun Congress of 1907.[50]

The Christ Seal and the True I of Man

On the same apocalyptic seal one finds the well-known Four Riders of the Apocalypse. They signify a fourfold relationship of the incarnating soul to the instrument of its physical body. One also sees there *the pentagram, hexagram and heptagram*. These were not in the biblical Apocalypse; they refer to the higher development of the human being, which leads him to becoming conscious of the etheric body, the astral body, and, finally, of the real I.

VII. WHICH BEING WAS ACTIVE AT THE BEGINNING AND END OF KALI YUGA?

Four beings have been indicated, and their deeds and the tasks set before humanity by these deeds have been described: Michael, Christ, Sorath and Ahriman. But a fifth event and its corresponding task has also been mentioned. This is the event of the year 1899 which marked the end of Kali Yuga and simultaneously, the beginning of a new Age of Light. On the one hand, this event clearly belongs to the series of the five, and yet at first glance it seems quite different from the other four. Rudolf Steiner did not directly specify a spiritual being in connection with it. Does this mean that the event of 1899 does *not* have to do with a being or beings? It would seem justified to raise the question.

The following considerations seek to contribute to an answer to this unavoidable question.

The small temporal cycles of about 350 years are all guided by seven spirits of the rank of archangels who each exercise the function of Time Spirit for a given period, and even bear concrete names — from Oriphiel to Michael. The larger epochs, which last 2,160 years each and stand above the smaller cycles, constituting a whole cultural epoch, are guided by mightier spirits; their scope of action goes far beyond that of the regents of the seven smaller Time Spirit cycles, which are embedded within that scope, as we have seen (see Fig 1, p. 12). The fifth post-Atlantean Epoch thus began with the activity of Samael, was followed by the activity of others of the seven Time Archangels, and will be followed by yet others after the present Age of Michael. Today we find ourselves in this sense, as already mentioned, in 5/7 — that is, in the seventh sub-cycle (ruled by Michael) of the fifth post-Atlantean Epoch. The spirits which guide the precessional culture epochs (each of 2,160 years) are also specific beings but yet—apart from one exception which will be mentioned later— without evident names.

A still longer cycle of time is that of 5,000 years, the Kali Yuga cycle. One who thinks in spiritual-scientific terms will obviously also have to seek out a specific impelling and guiding spiritual being for this cycle, which is so decisive for the whole evolution of human consciousness. It is inconceivable that the activities of the two smaller cycles (c. 350 and 2,160 years) are embedded in a larger cycle, without this cycle itself being guided by a particular very high, powerful being. The question is therefore not *whether* there is a being behind the event of 1899, but *which one*? Who is this being? Did Steiner at least leave any clues? Yes he did, even if only in an indirect form.

An Indication in the Oslo Folk Souls Lecture Cycle

In the seventh lecture of the Oslo lecture cycle on the Folk Souls in June 1910 (GA 121), Steiner describes developments of various spiritual beings to whom he had already referred in previous lectures, especially those of the Folk Spirits, who are of the rank of archangels. First, the Folk Spirit of the ancient Indian epoch went through a development which made him the leading Time Spirit of that epoch. That means that his scope of activity stretched over an entire epoch of 2,160 years. Through this he was raised to the rank of Arché [one of the Archai—*tr.*], 'who worked intuitively on the great teachers of India, the Holy Rishis, who were able to accomplish their high mission in the manner already described, because of what they had received from this exalted, significant spirit. This Time Spirit worked on for a long time', Steiner went on, 'when the people who lived north of ancient India [the ancient Persians] were still under the leadership of the [Persian] archangel.' And now follows a sentence that is of great weight for our present question: 'After the Time Spirit of India had fulfilled his mission *he was raised to the leadership of the entire evolution of post-Atlantean mankind.*'

Post-Atlantean mankind develops through seven cultural epochs, each lasting 2,160 years, in total 15,000 years. The spiritual radius of activity of the single Indian Time Spirit therefore encompasses six times more than the Time Spirit of a single epoch. He also encompasses a period three times longer than that of Kali Yuga, which itself lasts longer than two cultural epochs. This being, who had been the earlier Folk and Time Spirit of India and who had risen to become the leading spirit of the entire post-Atlantean Epoch, we may regard as the regent or creator of Kali Yuga. But he did not work alone but in consensus with still higher beings. Above all, this seems to have been the case in regard to *the end* of Kali Yuga.

The End of Kali Yuga—a Demand by the Gods

On 5 November 1912 Rudolf Steiner pointed to 'beings of the higher hierarchies ... who in the spiritual worlds had to bring about the end of Kali Yuga', for 'they needed something [...] which occurred on our Earth'. What did they need? 'They needed the fact [...], that ideas about this change [i.e. the end of Kali Yuga] would live in human souls.' Specifically, this meant: 'Just as a human being needs a brain on the physical plane in order to develop a consciousness, so the beings of the higher hierarchies need human thoughts which reflect the things that the higher hierarchies do.'[51] In saying this, Rudolf Steiner points to the hierarchical cosmic necessity for the development of spiritual science. Only a superficial view would see it as an accident that in August 1899, Steiner published an essay in which he inaugurated his later theosophical-spiritual-scientific activities by linking in that essay to Goethe's *Fairy Tale of the Green Snake and the Beautiful Lily.*[52]

*

So behind the consciousness-forming event of 1899, a particular spiritual being can be found as could be shown with the other four events (of 1879, 1933, 1998 and today). This being was acting, as it were, at the behest of those higher hierarchies which Steiner mentioned on 5 November 1912. We can add that all four cosmic events not only fall in the Age of Michael but also in that of the leading spirit 'of the entire evolution of post-Atlantean humanity'.

Vidar—the Leading Spirit of the Fifth Post-Atlantean Epoch

This high spiritual being who had risen through an enormously intensive development was already preparing *during* the Age of Kali Yuga the development of the new clairvoyance of the future, which would be led by thought, a new metamorphosed product of the 'pearl' of the ancient clairvoyance. The new clairvoyance will have to overcome the remains of the old clairvoyance. To this end, an archangel who has become the guiding spirit of the fifth cultural epoch is working in complete harmony. *This* spirit is the former archangel of the Germanic peoples, who was 'educated' both by the former Greek Folk Spirit, who then became the Time Spirit of exoteric Christianity, and also by the former Roman Folk Spirit, who in the later Roman epoch likewise exercised the functions of a Time Spirit, as described by Steiner in the seventh lecture of the *Folk Souls* cycle (1910). As the third element in his 'education', the leading spirit of the fifth post-Atlantean Epoch also has to come to a kind of compromise with the old Time Spirit of Egypt, who in the meantime has been 'raised to a certain rank within the Spirits of Form'. This is understandable when one recalls that certain 'mirror impulses', transformations of impulses from the third cultural epoch, must necessarily appear in our fifth cultural epoch.

The Germanic-Scandinavian mythology points to the spirit of the fifth epoch through the figure of 'Vidar', who has to christianize all the ancient clairvoyance that is incorporated in the Fenris Wolf. The picture that results is a grandiose harmony of tasks in the impulses of the former Indian Time Spirit with those of the present guiding spirit of the fifth cultural epoch ('Vidar') and with the intentions of Michael. This view of the deeply decisive year of development, 1899, can show us how the guides of three different Time Spirits' spheres work together on the new, true clairvoyance which opens up for us the experience of the Etheric Christ.

With regard to Kali Yuga which ended in 1899, we can end here with a remark by Sigismund von Gleich, according to which not only the end of Kali Yuga but also its beginning (3101 BC) fell in an Age of Michael; furthermore, the exact middle of Kali Yuga occurred in the year 601 BC which likewise also fell in an Age of Michael! These facts naturally lend to the event of 1899, as it were, an additional Michaelic value.[53]

VIII. LOOKING AHEAD TO THE NEXT TIME SPIRIT PERIODS WITHIN THE AGE OF PISCES

The Fourth Sorath Attack

Around the year AD 2200, Michael, Time Spirit of the Sun, will give way to Oriphiel, a Saturn spirit. At that future time a very particular polarization within mankind, already discernible today, will be approaching its peak: a polarity between the development of an individualism based on thought and ethics, and one which inclines to a life hostile to thought and which does away with everything individual. In April 1916 Rudolf Steiner referred to a general 'prohibition of thinking' which was then looming, and which would not be propagated directly as such, but which would be installed de facto through all kinds of indirect methods.[54]

But let us at first remain focused on the Sun Demon. He first appeared in human development in the Christian Era (666); that was in an Age of Zachariel, a Jupiter epoch. The second sorathic attack followed at the time of the Templars (1332) — that is, during that Age of Samael, which also gave to the whole fifth post-Atlantean Epoch of the Fishes (Pisces) its underlying character (see p. 11f.). Today, we are still living through the aura of the third sorathic attack (1998). The *fourth* sorathic attack in the Christian Era will follow after a further 666 years, so its focus will be on and around the year 2664; this fourth focus will therefore be in the Age of *Anael*, which begins around 2570. The last sorathic attack in the present Piscean Epoch will occur in 3330, relatively soon after the beginning of the next Age of Raphael (3260–3610).

The Beginning of the Sixth Post-Atlantean Epoch in an Age of Raphael

The *last years* of the next Raphael Age, however, will reach into the beginnings of the next post-Atlantean cultural epoch, which in accordance with the precession of the spring equinox, will commence in the year 3573. In other words: whereas the fourth post-Atlantean cultural Epoch began under the sign of Gabriel (Moon), and the fifth under the sign of Samael (Mars), the sixth will begin under the sign of *Raphael* (Mercury). As, for example, Samael gave and continues to give the underlying tone to the whole fifth post-Atlantean Epoch, Raphael will do this for the sixth epoch. The coming Age of Raphael will therefore, on the one hand, close the fifth post-Atlantean Epoch and on the other, lead in the sixth epoch. The fundamental task of the fifth epoch will, in a certain sense, come to an end in this Age of Raphael; that task is, as we have seen, the confrontation with evil, whereas the problem of *birth and death* was the task of the fourth epoch, which began in an Age of Gabriel. What the basic task of the *sixth* post-Atlantean Epoch will be was not given to us in a similar way in any basic formula by Rudolf Steiner. But we can deduce something from the fact that the epoch will begin with a Raphael impulse. An Age of Raphael stands under the impulse of sickness and healing: that is the basic polarity of such an age. One can think of the poetry created in the last Age of Raphael, which went back to the impulses of the Grail. The whole of Wolfram von Eschenbach's *Parzival* can be seen from this perspective. It is the drama of the *sickness* of Amfortas and of its *healing* by Parzival.

The Healing of the Wounds of Evil

But let us look again at the basic task of the fifth post-Atlantean Epoch, which will come to its relative conclusion in a future Raphael Age. By then, the forces of evil will have caused many wounds. But for an understanding of evil one can in such an epoch look to the cosmic healer of all polarities, to Christ, who will prepare Himself to appear to human beings in the sixth post-Atlantean Epoch in the *astral world*. A precondition for this, of course, is that they take up the impulses which Christ is sending to them in His present etheric appearance.

Assuming that this precondition is met, then even those deep wounds suffered by entire peoples will undergo a certain healing at the beginning of the sixth epoch. We can think, for example, of the lasting damage done to the Slavic peoples, and also to Hungary, by the Bolshevism inspired by Sorath. In the sixth epoch the Slavic peoples will actually become those who lead the way.

They will only be able to fulfil their task, however, in so far as the wounds are actually healed. The battle for the heart of Slavic culture which commenced soon after the beginning of the fifth post-Atlantean Epoch will continue until the end of the epoch, and will even culminate in the age that will close off this fifth epoch — namely, in that Raphael Age which will see yet another sorathic attack. But then, strengthened through their spiritual defence against the repeated attacks of Sorath, there will be spiritually developed individualities who will be able to accomplish major acts of healing of the wounds that will have been inflicted on the folk substance of the Slavic peoples. In this sense, it is a sign of great hope that the sixth, Slavic cultural Epoch will begin during an Age of Raphael.

This will also be the time in which the Maitreya Bodhisattva, the rising successor to the last Buddha [Gautama], will become the bearer of the magically healing *Word*. 'The Maitreya Buddha will speak words', said Steiner on 21 September 1911, 'which will through their magical power become moral impulses in the people who hear them.'[55]

A Remark on the Various Time Spirit Rhythms

We have established that the great post-Atlantean Epochs of 2,160 years are always introduced by a different Time Spirit who is active for about 350 years. The fifth epoch was introduced by Samael, and the sixth will be introduced by Raphael. The great rhythms determined by precessional movement (2,160 years) and the rhythms of the seven smaller Time Spirits (about 350 years) do not align exactly. That *would* be the case if each of the smaller Time Spirit rhythms were exactly 308 years — a seventh of 2,160 years. Rudolf Steiner recorded this number in a note book relating to the Apocalypse lectures to the priests of the Christian

Community. Since the actual periods of activity are 30–40 years longer than 308 years, there is an overlap of two Time Spirit spheres, the larger (2,160 years) and the middle one (about 350 years). The beginning of the larger epochs therefore does not always begin in *the same* smaller epoch. Furthermore, in the case of the 350 year-long periods apportioned to the seven Archangels of Time, it is only a matter of an average periodicity, from which there can again be smaller deviations. The average values given by Trithemius von Sponheim and his pupil Agrippa von Nettesheim, according to an entry in one of Rudolf Steiner's notebooks on 18 August 1924, are given with the following small variations: '1879–1510 Gabriel / 1510–1190 Samael / 1190–850 Raphael / 850–500 Zachariel / 500–150 Anael / 150–200 BC Oriphiel'.[56]

In Steiner's reckoning too, the evident norm is 350 years (Oriphiel, Anael, and Zachariel); Raphael ruled for 340 years, while Samael ruled for about 30 years less than the norm, and Gabriel on the other hand about 20 years longer than it.

As cast-iron, measured and regular as is the course of precession which is determinant in the case of the great epochs, the rhythms of the smaller Time Spirits are elastic. This is shown by the fact that the various spheres of the Time Spirits do not relate to each other in a mechanistic, rigid fashion, but sound together in a lively manner. The light variations in the smaller periods bring a wonderful liveliness into the interplay between the smaller and the larger Time Spirit spheres. Just as a good human orchestra is not directed with a rigid conductor's baton, neither is the orchestra of cosmic and human development. The cosmic conductors work, like a good earthly conductor, with a timely, a-rhythmic sense, with accelerandos and rallentandos.

The Planetary Demons, according to Agrippa von Nettesheim

Just as the Sun — seen in the Ptolemaic sense as the central planet of our system — has its demon, which precisely in our Michael Age has come to be of great significance and effectiveness and will continue to be so, the other cosmic bodies in our solar system also possess their 'Anti-spirit' or demon. The afore-mentioned Agrippa von Nettesheim, to whom, along with Paracelsus, Steiner set a memorial in his *Die Mystik im Aufgange des neuzeitlichen Geisteslebens und ihr Verhältnis zur modernen Weltanschauung* (GA 7) [Mysticism at the Dawn of Modern Spiritual Life and Its Relation to the Modern Worldview], wrote in his book *Die geheime Philosophie* [Occult Philosophy], published only a few days before his death: the Saturn demon is called Zazel, the demon of Jupiter Hismael; Barzabel is named the demon of Mars, Sorath the Sun demon, Kedemel the Venus demon, Taphthartharath the demon of Mercury, and finally, Hasmodai, the Moon demon. In a Dornach lecture after the Christmas Conference (January 1924) Rudolf Steiner referred to this old spiritual cosmology and drew attention to the fact that it also included a nameless *Earth demon*.[57] That Steiner was well-acquainted with the spiritual cosmology and the demonology of Agrippa is clear from a number of Steiner's esoteric Class lessons in which spiritual beings such as Azael, Azazel, or Mehazel are mentioned, beings to whom he otherwise hardly ever referred.[58] The last-named here refer to beings whose activities are entirely beneficent and who aid human beings to come to real self-knowledge.

Is it to be expected that in future epochs, not only the Sun demon with his rhythm of 666 years will play a role in the shaping of history but also the demons of the other planetary spheres? No being exists who remains forever inactive. The question is only intended to be posed here, not answered.

IX. THE DEVELOPMENT OF MANKIND IN THE COURSE OF A COSMIC YEAR

From the Last to the Present Epoch of the Fishes (Pisces)
We are living in an age of great crises and small thoughts. To the great crises belong less the worldwide financial and economic crisis or the current world situation threatened as it is by war than the epidemic absence of *spiritual* ways of thinking about the world; to the small thoughts belong less the fixed idea of 'constant, lasting growth', around which so many people gather as though round a magic totem, than the widespread idea that humanity gets along without spirit and also progresses without it.

Great crises can only be overcome with great thoughts. Such great thoughts first require a *comprehensive* concept of development which includes not only growth but also the lawful destruction of what has grown. Spiritual science speaks of evolution and involution.[59] To such thoughts belong, furthermore, the great fundamental ideas of spiritual science which can teach us how to set the events of a day, a year, or even a century into the broad vistas of world-historical perspectives.

Development as the Interplay of Destruction and Construction
In the course of a year on both large and small scales, nature brings about a wonderful balance between the two poles of all development — despite climate catastrophes, earthquakes, and volcanic eruptions. Such a balance is as a rule never striven for in today's financial theories.

Steiner's idea that a piece of paper money with an end date, which would lose its value at a particular point in time, chases away fear and fright. But people do not believe in the possibility of a regulated revaluation or new creation of lost value. It is as if they were to fear in autumn that there would be no new seeds, growth, or flowers.

But phases of growth also follow those of decay in the development of mankind as a whole. Lemuria emerged – and was destroyed in a fiery catastrophe. Atlantis arose and then in a watery catastrophe sank to the bottom of the ocean. Our post-Atlantean Epoch will in only a few thousand years experience its downfall in a catastrophe of the air – only to make way for a new development that will take place under changed conditions.[60]

The Cosmic Year

A still greater, more creative world thought that embraces the destruction and re-creation of whole continents and cultures is literally present in the stars: it is the cosmic year which is formed by the movement of the vernal point of the Sun (backwards along the zodiacal circle) through 25,920 years. That this macrocosmic thought rhythm permeates everything in the world and therefore also the microcosmic nature of man is shown by the fact that the human being takes on average 18 breaths a minute, which is 25,920 breaths in 24 hours! This is the same number – in the one case as a cosmic year, and in the other as a human day. The twelve zodiac signs form the cosmic dial for the twelve 'months' of a cosmic year.

Our fifth post-Atlantean Epoch lies, as mentioned numerous times already, in the sign of the Fishes (Pisces). The first post-Atlantean Epoch began in the sign of the Crab (Cancer), and the entire epoch will end in the sign of the Goat (Capricorn) in the seventh epoch, which will lead to the emergence of a completely new Great Epoch. In the Apocalypse this is called the time of the 'seals'. This will be the sixth Great Earth Epoch. What is known as the Flood in the mythologies of many peoples – the sinking of Atlantis – occurred in the sign of the Lion (Leo); the beginning of the Atlantean epoch took place in the sign of the Waterbearer (Aquarius).

Physical Autonomy in the Last Epoch of the Fishes (Pisces)

When was mankind last in an epoch of the Fishes (Pisces)? That was in the seventh age of the Lemurian Epoch. Since that time the whole of mankind has developed for exactly one cosmic year; today, seen from a cosmic perspective, it stands exactly where it was at the endpoint of its development in the Lemurian Epoch, only at a higher level. Rudolf Steiner pointed this out in two lectures in Dornach on 9 and 10 July 1921.[61]

Naturally, the human being was present in still earlier epochs in spirit and soul. Spiritual science traces the original physical emergence of the human being back to the first developmental condition of human cosmic development, which is called 'Old Saturn'.[62]

What was special about the entire development of the human race that took place in the last epoch of Lemuria? The actual *earthly* emergence of man occurred in that epoch.

All of us descended from relatively ethereal earth-air-water bodies down on to the condensed Earth. This was our expulsion from paradise. We set foot on the hard Earth for the first time. In Sri Lanka, one of the coastal regions of ancient Lemuria, a legend that is still extant today tells of how Adam's first footfall was on the sacred mountain named after him — Adam's Peak.[63]

This took place in the last of the seven Lemurian epochs, which stood under the sign of the Fishes (Pisces). In traditional astrology, there is a relationship between the signs of the zodiac and twelve parts or areas of the human body. Pisces corresponds to the feet. In the last Lemurian Epoch, the last Piscean Epoch before our own, the human being literally set his feet on the firm earth for the first time. This was also the time in which the spark of the I was bestowed upon him by the Spirits of Form.

Development during the Atlantean Epoch

The Atlantean Period as a whole was dedicated to the formation and further condensation of the form of the body, which became more and more suited to the development of the I. This principally came to expression in the upright posture, which the human race in the earlier Lemurian Epoch had still lacked. The Atlantean formation of the body followed the bestowal of the I upon the soul, whose bearer and servant the body was increasingly to become. In this process, for most human beings sexual fertilization remained a matter shrouded in a deep unconsciousness until far into the Atlantean epoch.

... and in the post-Atlantean Epoch

If the development in the Atlantean Epoch was that of the relationship of the *physical* and the soul elements of the human being, in the post-Atlantean Epoch after the great catastrophe, there followed a powerful shift of accent: now the *soul element* in this relationship was more emphasized in a particular way, beginning in the etheric body in the Indian Epoch up to the development of the Consciousness Soul in our present Piscean Epoch which, as already mentioned, began in AD 1413 and will continue until the year 3573.

Body, Soul — and Spirit

In a lecture on 9 July 1921 Rudolf Steiner drew a sketch on a board. It can perhaps serve to make more clearly understandable the threefold process of development of the human being, which he was describing only in outline. [My own comments are in square brackets — TM]

The sketch shows the passage through the zodiac since the last Lemurian Epoch. The epochs from the last Lemurian Epoch until the last Atlantean Epoch are lightly indicated, while the four completed epochs and the still uncompleted fifth post-Atlantean Epoch are shown by darker lines. Steiner commented, evidently referring to this sketch:

> During the passage of the vernal point through the Fishes human beings were hardly in the physical form in which they are [today] (sketched lightly).[64] Here [all seven Atlantean epochs are meant] the human form is becoming ever more physical. And here [the lecturer apparently pointed to the darkly sketched lines from the Indian Epoch to our time] soul development begins, and here [the present Piscean Epoch], it returns to where it once was in relation to its physical formation.

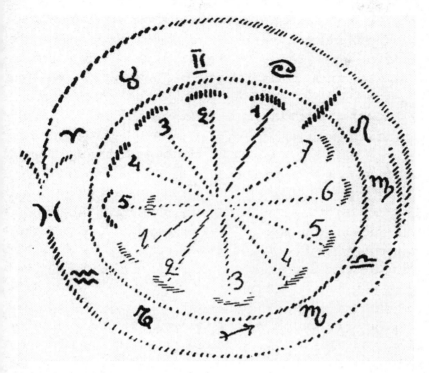

*Fig 7   World Development from the Lemurian until the Present
Piscean Epoch*

And more precisely: 'The zodiac signs of the Fishes, the Water-bearer, the Goat, the Centaur, the Scorpion, the Scales until here, the Virgin (sketched lightly) correspond to the formation of the human physical form; and only these upper zodiac signs [from the Lion to the Ram] correspond to the formation of the soul being of Man.'

In other words, at the end of the Cosmic Year that began with the Lemurian Epoch, the human being was 'formed' with respect to his body and soul. The new current Piscean Epoch leads him to the portal of the spirit. That is the spiritual significance of our own Piscean epoch.

The development of our body and soul since the last Piscean epoch was taken care of by higher beings. It happened, as a rule, without our having to do anything consciously and freely. One can speak of *the education of the human being* in body and soul. With the development of the Consciousness Soul, however, the soul development comes to a certain conclusion. The education of the human race guided by higher beings is now to be replaced by a completely new form of development: the self-education of the I that has become free. Now, it is a matter of taking up in full consciousness the sparks of the I in the soul—which means the sparks of the spirit in us—and of unfolding them continuously; and doing this in freedom and with complete autonomy.

Spiritual Autonomy and the Birth of Spiritual Science
In the Lemurian Piscean Epoch we achieved physical autonomy on Earth for the first time—with the help of the Gods. In our present Piscean Epoch, we are to learn to stand on our own feet spiritually. Spiritual science made its appearance in the world in order to facilitate this step forward from physical to spiritual autonomy, and to guide it in the right direction. It represents the means of cultivating this autonomy under the sign of a comprehensive knowledge of the world and of oneself and on the basis of a true individualism. That, in a zodiacal-cosmic sense, is its world-historical mission. If it is not taken up, the autonomy of the human soul and spirit threaten to harden into egoism, which only furthers 'the war of all against all'. This war is already in its grotesque beginnings today, and it will ultimately lead to the downfall of our post-Atlantean Epoch.

Through the adoption of spiritual science in the present Piscean Epoch, seeds of new growth will be laid for the period after the downfall of our post-Atlantean Epoch. To these seeds belongs the understanding of evil as a fundamental task of the fifth post-Atlantean Epoch, and that ultimately means the *positive* function of evil, as this small book has attempted to show. Every human being is free to ignore spiritual science and thus contribute towards the downfall of the present great Earth Epoch, or else to take it up through the application of his or her understanding and reason and thus to contribute to the construction of the next great Earth Epoch.

X. CONCLUDING THOUGHTS

A question that could arise in regard to what has been presented in this book is: why should we pay so much attention to all the disharmony, all the opposition in the world and among human beings, when the highest spirits themselves exist in absolute harmony? Why did they create such disharmony, conflict, and wars in the world in the first place? One answer is: because opposition is the *motor* of development. All development in time is achieved through the prevalence of great polarities: day and night, winter and summer, man and woman, good and evil—to name but a few. This, considered in the broadest sense, is how great Mother Nature works. This is the meaning of Heraclitus' saying: 'War is the father of all things.'

However, the human being is here to *harmonize* the polarities, not to create new ones. The latter is the responsibility of the wise guidance of the world, which has placed responsibility for the former into the hands of mankind.

In this way, through a gradual overcoming of all polarities, an intensification of human capacities is achieved that could not be arrived at in any other way. But polarities can only be overcome by one who has his own spiritual centre above them, who, as it were, seeks to orient himself to the pole star of the absolute good, of absolute harmony. Whoever remains bound up in the error of the number two, of duality, can only create further dualities, further polarities, and can never mediate between polarities, let alone unite them in a higher harmony. This is why it is so important that more and more people free themselves from the mental prison of binary thinking, which, however, underlies all of today's computer technology. Mankind has certainly created countless things that are new and great, and yet few have learned to count their way from two to three.

In the three rests the unity of all polarities, the *coincidentia oppositorum,* as Nicolàs of Cusa called it. It is the infinite eternal in which all polarities are resolved.

The thoughts about the strongest of these polarities which have been presented in this small book have not been put forward out of any love for these polarities or oppositions, or out of any false fascination for them, but in consideration of the source from which they all stem, and from which alone they will all be able to find their future reconciliation.

The fundamental polarity of our time is that between good and evil. The *higher* Good, which precedes the polarity between good and evil, is the actual, true Good, or, if one prefers, *the truly good Good.* Outside it is the 'good' that remains stuck in the binary of good and evil — a weak, if not to say a 'bad' good.

Rudolf Steiner wanted to direct the sense of the listener or reader to this higher Good when, in his Mystery Drama *The Soul's Probation,* he spoke of the deepest riddling question of our time in the simple words of a fairy tale. Let these words suffice to close our aphoristic considerations.

> *From where does evil come?*
> There once lived a man,
> Who thought much about the things of the world.
> It racked his brain the most
> When he wanted to know the origin of evil.
> But he could not provide himself with an answer.
> 'The world is made by God', he said to himself,
> 'And God can only have in Himself the Good.
> How can evil people come from the Good?'
> He thought and thought but all in vain;
> The answer would not show itself.
> Then it happened one day that the brooder
> On his way espied a tree
> In conversation with an axe.
> The axe said to the tree:
> 'What you can't do, *I can.*
> I can cut you down, but you can't do the same to me.'
> The tree replied to the conceited axe:
> 'A year ago a man took the wood

With which he made your shaft
From my body with another axe.'
And when the man heard those words,
A thought came into his mind
Which he could not put clearly into words
But which fully answered the question:
How can evil stem from good?

Notes

GA = *Gesamtausgabe* or Collected Works. See Bibliography on p. 92.

1. The discussion here is based on the spiritual-astronomical determinations in spiritual science. The beginning of such an epoch always falls in the middle of an astronomical Zodiac sign. See Elisabeth Vreede, *Anthroposophie und Astronomie*, Freiburg im Breisgau, p. 113ff.

2. The collection was titled *Durch den Geist zur Wirklichkeits-Erkenntnis der Menschheitsrätsel von Rudolf Steiner — Nicht im Buchhandel, Liebesgabe für deutsche Kriegsgefangene* [Towards an Understanding of the Reality of the Riddle of Man through the Spirit by Rudolf Steiner — Not for sale in bookshops, a Gift of Love for German POWs], published by the Philosophisch-Anthroposophische Verlag in Berlin.

3. See p. 86f., where this fairy tale is printed.

4. GA 273.

5. See especially the lecture of 16 April 1906, GA 96 and of 4 September 1906, GA 95.

6. See R. Steiner, 'Die Evolution vom Gesichtspunkt des Wahrhaftigen' [Evolution from the Perspective of Truthfulness], lecture of 14 November 1911, GA 132.

7. Adelheid Petersen, *Welthistorische Zusammenhänge und Inkarnationsgeheimnisse in Rudolf Steiners Mysteriendramen* [World-historical Relationships and Secrets of Incarnation in Rudolf Steiner's Mystery Dramas], Dornach, 1957.

8. Adelheid Petersen, 'Dornach in the Years 1914/1915', in *Errinnerungen an Rudolf Steiner*, Stuttgart 1979, p. 184ff.

9. Lecture of 22 March 1909, in the cycle *Geisteswissenschaftliche Menschenkunde*, GA 107.

10. See W.J. Stein, 'Weltgeschichte im Lichte des konkreten Zeitgeist-Wirkens', in *Der Europäer*, Vol. 12, No. 9/10, July/August 2008, p. 3ff. The occultist Trithemius von Sponheim (1462–1516) discussed by Stein here reckons with a regency of 354 years, which R. Steiner essentially confirmed. See also p. 76.

11. Ernst Bindel, *Die geistigen Grundlagen der Zahlen* [The Spiritual Foundations of Numbers], Stuttgart 1980.
12. Rudolf Steiner, 1 November 1919, GA 191.
13. See T.H. Meyer, *Rudolf Steiner's Core Mission*, Temple Lodge, 2010.
14. Quoted in *Was in der anthroposophischen Gesellschaft vorgeht*, 7 September 1980, p. 147.
15. See T.H. Meyer, *The Bodhisattva Question*, Temple Lodge, 2010.
16. These notes were published and commented on for the first time in *Der Europäer*, Dec./Jan. 2010/11: 'Rudolf Steiner gives in Stockholm the first lectures on the Return of Christ in the Etheric'. Marie Steiner's notes can be seen in Figs. 2 and 3.
17. See T.H. Meyer, *Reality, Truth and Evil, Facts, Questions, and Perspectives on September 11, 2001*, Temple Lodge, 2005.
18. See *Der Meditationsweg der Michaelschule*, Basel, 2nd edn., 2012, p. 246f.
19. See Charles Kovacs, *The Apocalypse in Rudolf Steiner's Lecture Series*, Floris Books, 2013. Also, p. 57.
20. See the essay 'Die Erkenntnis des Bösen und die Inkarnation Ahrimans im Westen' [The Understanding of Evil and the Incarnation of Ahriman in the West], in T.H. Meyer, *Von Moses zu 9/11, Weltgeschichtliche Ereignisse und geisteswissenschaftliche Kernimpulse* [From Moses to 9/11, World-historical Events and Key Spiritual-scientific Impulses — untranslated], Basel, 2010, p. 161ff.
21. For example, in the karma lecture given in Arnhem on 18 July 1924, GA 240, where he spoke of a spiritual 'renewal' which 'would lead even what is intellectual up into the spiritual'.
22. *Briefe von Rudolf Steiner* [Letters from Rudolf Steiner], Vol. II, Dornach, 1953, appended to the letter of 16 August 1902.
23. Lecture of 13 January 1924, GA 233a; emphasis TM.
24. W.J. Stein/Rudolf Steiner — *Dokumentation eines wegweisenden Zusammenwirkens* [W.J. Stein/Rudolf Steiner — Documentation of a Pioneering Collaboration], edited by T.H. Meyer, Dornach, 1985, p. 284 [untranslated].
25. Steiner spoke in this sense on 29 May 1913 in Helsinki of the 'pearl of clairvoyance' in sense-free thinking (GA 146). See also T.H. Meyer, *Clairvoyance and Consciousness*, Temple Lodge, 2012.
26. 17 August 1918, GA 183.
27. Rudolf Steiner spoke in his early lectures of the 'ten-or eight-

petalled' lotus flowers; it appears to be the only one of all the lotus flowers where the functions fluctuate in a narrow spectrum.

28. O.W. Barth Verlag, 3rd edn., Freiburg-im-Breisgau, 1974.
29. See, for example, the key lecture of 13 October 1923 in GA 229.
30. Basel, 1992. English edition: *When the Storm Comes/A Moment in the Blossom Kingdom*, Clairview Books 2001.
31. *Sie erlebten Christus, Berichte aus einer Untersuchung des religionssoziologischen Instituts Stockholm* [They experienced Christ, Reports from an Investigation by the Institute for Religion and Sociology], publ. by G. Hillerdal and B. Gustafsson, Basel, 2nd edn., 1980.
32. GA 367.
33. See *Die Evolution vom Gesichtspunkte des Wahrhaftigen*, GA 132, Lecture of 14 November 1911.
34. 22 March 1909, GA 107.
35. 11 October 1918, GA 184.
36. Goethe, *Dichtung und Wahrheit* [Poetry and Truth], Part III, Book 15.
37. *Das Evangelium des Judas* [The Gospel of Judas], ed. by R. Kasser, M. Meyer and G. Wurst, Washington, D.C., 2006.
38. GA 268.
39. Facebook item, Archive of Perseus Verlag. See *Der Europäer*, Vol. 18, Nos 1, 2–3 and 4.
40. From T.H. Meyer, *D.N. Dunlop – A Man of Our Time*, 2nd enlarged edn., 2014, p. 208; emphasis TM.
41. GA 346.
42. Rudolf Steiner, 2 November 1919, GA 191.
43. GA 191.
44. See the chapter 'Some effects of initiation', in *Knowledge of the Higher Worlds – How Is It Achieved?*, GA 10.
45. Rudolf Steiner, *Geisteswissenschaft und soziale Frage* [Spiritual Science and the Social Question], GA 34.
46. See *Der Meditationsweg der Michaelschule in neunzehn Stufen*, Vol. 1 and enlarged volume 2, Basel, 3rd edn., 2013.
47. On *Zum Irrwahn der Zweizahl* [The Delusion of the Number Two], see R. Steiner, GA 194, 21 November 1919.
48. See, e.g., Heinrich Cornelius Agrippa von Nettesheim, *Die magischen Werke* [The Magical Works], Wiesbaden, 1982.
49. GA 104a. The following citations are from the same lecture.

50. See the loose leaf plates in GA 284.

51. GA 141.

52. Rudolf Steiner, *Goethes geheime Offenbarung in seinem Märchen* [Goethe's Secret Revelation in His Fairy Tale] essay, 1899, single edition.

53. Sigismund von Gleich, *Marksteine der Kulturgeschichte* [Milestones in Cultural History], Vols I–IV, Stuttgart, 3rd edn., 1982, p. 26ff [untranslated].

54. 4 April 1916, GA 167.

55. GA 130.

56. See GA 243.

57. See the lecture of 11 January 1924 in GA 233a.

58. See, for example, certain esoteric lessons before the First World War, in GA 266a and 266b.

59. See T.H. Meyer, *Wegmarken im Leben Rudolf Steiners und in der Entwicklung der Anthroposophie* [Milestones in the Life of Rudolf Steiner and in the Development of Anthroposophy], Basel, 2012. Forthcoming: Temple Lodge, 2015.

60. See Rudolf Steiner's lecture of 13 May 1921, in GA 204.

61. GA 205.

62. See *Occult Science – An Outline*, GA 13.

63. See Laurence Oliphant, 'The Ascent of Adam's Peak on Sri Lanka' in T.H. Meyer (ed.), *Laurence Oliphant, When a Stone Begins to Roll, Notes of an Adventurer, Diplomat & Mystic*, Lindisfarne, Great Barrington 2011.

64. In the transcript of the lecture in GA 205, p. 167, this is erroneously rendered as 'sketched darkly'.

Bibliography of Works by Rudolf Steiner

The following volumes are cited in this book. Where relevant, published editions of equivalent English translations are given. (The works of Rudolf Steiner are listed with the volume numbers of the complete works in German—GA—as published by Rudolf Steiner Verlag, Dornach, Switzerland.)

10	*Knowledge of the Higher Worlds / How to Know Higher Worlds*
13	*Occult Science / An Outline of Esoteric Science*
34	*Lucifer-Gnosis, Grundlegende Aufsätze zur Anthroposophie und Berichte aus den Zeitschriften 'Luzifer' und 'Lucifer-Gnosis' 1903–1908*
95	*Founding a Science of the Spirit*
96	*Original Impulses for the Science of the Spirit*
104a	*Reading the Pictures of the Apocalypse*
107	*Disease, Karma and Healing*
130	*Esoteric Christianity and the Mission of Christian Rosenkreutz*
132	*Inner Realities of Evolution*
141	*Between Death and Rebirth*
146	*The Bhagavad Gita and the West*
167	*Gegenwärtiges und Vergangenes im Menschengeiste*
184	*Die Polarität von Dauer und Entwickelung im Menschenleben*
191	*Die geistigen Hintergründe der sozialen Frage, Band III*
194	*Die Sendung Michaels*
204	*Materialism and the Task of Anthroposophy*
205	*Menschenwerden, Weltenseele und Weltengeist – Erster Teil*
233a	*Rosicrucianism and Initiation*
240	*Karmic Relationships Vol. VI + VIII*
243	*True and False Paths in Spiritual Investigation*
266/1	*Esoteric Lessons, 1904–1909*
266/2	*Esoteric Lessons, 1910–1912*
273	*Geisteswissenschaftliche Erläuterungen zu Goethes 'Faust'*
284	*Occult Seals and Columns*
346	*The Book of Revelation and the Work of the Priest*

All English-language titles are available via Rudolf Steiner Press, UK (www.rudolfsteinerpress.com) or SteinerBooks, USA (www.steinerbooks.org)